Another Paradise
by **Sayan Kent**

First full production performed on 12 March 2009 at Manchester Contact Theatre

SUBSEQUENT TOUR
16 March – Newcastle Live Theatre
17 – March Stockton Arc
19-21 March – Leeds West Yorkshire Playhouse
24-28 March – Plymouth Theatre Royal (Drum)
31 March-4 April – Coventry Belgrade Theatre
7-9 March & 14-18 April – London Vanbrugh Theatre
23-24 April – London Rich Mix

Introduction

Another Paradise is set in Leamington Spa at a time when biometric Identity Cards are compulsory in a world in which humans are qualified by their digital status as stored in the National Identity Central Database. It is a perfect state. But then there is Coventry…

I started to write this play a few years ago when the identity card debate began to hot up. It was becoming blatantly clear that huge computer systems were unstable, unmanageable and ridiculously expensive but still the government was pushing ahead with its plan to eventually get the whole population's biometric identities on to a national computer database. It struck me as absurd and slightly hilarious but also worrying for the sinister idealism which lay behind the proposals. Whether or not the identity card scheme is to our 'benefit' is beside the point. The potential for things to go wrong is too great to ignore. Once we're on this huge database the word privacy will no longer mean what it used to. Our every move could potentially be monitored, whether we are applying for a mortgage or buying a cup of coffee.

Our personal information will be managed by the same people in government departments who have, in the recent past, casually lost the data of thousands of people. Ethically, what does it actually mean to have all our personal information at the fingertips of a civil servant? Does that violate our individuality, who we are, what we are? Does it make a mockery of our sense of freedom? What would happen to those people who didn't qualify for full citizenship but still reside here? The identity card debate raises fundamental questions about our civil liberties and human rights. Who are the real beneficiaries of this scheme? Not the general population. Somebody will be making a lot of money out it, legally, let alone illegally; the identity fraudsters will be having a field day. Identity theft is a growing problem and hackers are never far behind the latest security; sometimes they are ahead of it.

Modern technology is a wonderful thing and our lives are the better for it but it can be unwisely used. Humans must be in control of the technology. In writing this play I wanted to look at what could happen when it is the other way round, when the biometric ID programme starts to go wrong. When the computer breaks down. When the people in control of our identities make mistakes. When identities are corrupted, lost, or stolen. And I wanted to do it in a humorous and entertaining way. For me this story is about the survival of humanity over misguided technology. Should the biometric identity card scheme go full steam ahead it would move us, as a nation, into surreal territory.

Sayan Kent

Another Paradise

kalí

by **Sayan Kent**

Abigail **Shelley King**
Fisher **Karen Mann**
Enoch **Chand Martinez**
Lisa, Michelle, Thomas Paine **Sarah Paul**
Marcus **Richard Rees**

Director **Janet Steel**
Set and Costume Design **Alice Hoult**
Video Design **Eva Auster**
Lighting Designer **Chris Corner**
Composer **Sayan Kent**

Company Stage Manager **Beth Hoare-Barnes**
Assistant Director and ASM **Jessica Thanki**
Rehearsal ASM **Sonam Nagewadia**

General Manager **Christopher Corner**
Press Representation **Anne Mayer**
Marketing **Mobius**
Graphic Design **Luke Wakeman**
Photography **Robert Workman and Robert Day**
Set built by **Factory Settings**

Kali would like to thank everyone at Manchester Contact Theatre for all their help and support with presenting *Another Paradise*.

The play was first presented in an earlier version at the 2008 Edinburgh Festival with Sarah Belcher, Karen Mann, Chand Martinez, Sakuntala Ramanee, Richard Rees and casting by Leila Bertrand.

Thanks to all those involved in developing *Another Paradise* and presenting the first reading at Kali's November 2007 *Giving Voice* season at Soho Theatre.

Kali is funded by Arts Council England

kali

Kali seeks out strong individual South Asian women writers who challenge our perceptions through original and thought provoking theatre. The company has established a reputation for presenting work that takes audiences on unpredictable journeys that entertain, excite and inspire.

Since its inception in 1990, Kali's connections within the South Asian community have made it a natural home for women who are seeking new ways to express and explore the issues and human interest stories of the Diaspora.

Kali aims to present the distinct perspective and experience of Asian women to people from all backgrounds and to celebrate that richness and diversity. No idea is too small, no statement too large. We actively encourage our writers and audience to reinvent and reshape the theatrical agenda.

Through our new writer development programmes, we provide core resources for writers new to the theatre through workshops, dramaturgical support and public readings.

Kali Theatre Co. 20 Rupert Street London W1D 6DF
020 7494 9100 info@kalitheatre.co.uk

Further information about Kali can be found at www.kalitheatre.co.uk

kali Ltd Co. No. 2583595 Registered Charity No. 1071733

Photographs by Robert Day and Bob Workman

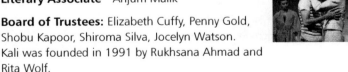

Biographies

Sayan Kent
Writer

Sayan Kent's other writing includes *Killing Wasps* (Soho Theatre, staged reading), *Housewife's Choice* (LBC radio), musical adaptations of *Silas Marner* (Belgrade, Coventry), *The Good Companions* (New Vic, Stoke) and three pantomimes. Sayan Kent originally trained as an actress at Rose Bruford and has worked extensively in regional theatre playing many leading roles. Her TV/Film work includes *Casualty*, *Coronation Street*, *EastEnders*, *Moveable Feasts*, *The Bill*, *The Big Battalions*, *The Paradise Club*, *Young Soul Rebels* and *Doctors*. Work as a theatre composer includes *Zameen* (ArtsTheatre/Kali), *Two* (Liverpool Royal Court), *Spangleguts* (London Bubble), *Paper Thin, Chaos, Sock 'em with Honey, Calcutta Kosher* (Kali), *Hound of the Baskervilles* (Paul Farrah Prods), *The Phantom Sausage* (Wolsey, Ipswich), *Turn of the Screw*, *Limestone Cowboy*, *Cinderella* (Coventry Belgrade), *Truckers* (Harrogate), *A Hard Rain* (Northampton), *Country* (New Vic Stoke), *Dinosaur Dreams* (Unicorn), *Hot Doris the Musical* (Oval House), *Factory Follies* (Croydon Warehouse), *72 Days* and *Bloody Elektra* (Oval House & Albany), *Good Companions, Silas Marner, Limestone Cowboy, Mother Goose, Dick Whittington, Aladdin*. She is also a director and lives in Coventry.

Shelley King
Abigail

Recent theatre: *Free Outgoing, The Crutch, Mohair, The Burrow* (Royal Court); *Man of Mode, Women of Troy, Little Clay Cart, Tartuffe* (RNT); *Bombay Dreams* (West End); *Besharam, Bezhti* (Birmingham Rep); *Orpheus, The Modern Husband, Ion* (Actors Touring Company); *Macbeth, Measure for Measure* (Theatre Unlimited); *Damian & Pythias* (Globe); *Troilus & Cressida, A Midsummer Night's Dream, Heer Ranjha, Danton's Death, Antigone* (Tara Arts); *Death and The Maiden* (Wolsey Ipswich); *Top Girls* (Royal Northampton). For Kali: *Paper Thin, Chaos, Calcutta Kosher, River On Fire*. Film & TV: *Code 46, Banglatown Banquet, A Secret Slave, See How They Run, Jewel In The Crown, King of the Ghetto, Tandoori Nights* (two series), *Angels* (two series) and numerous soaps. There have also been many enjoyable hours of short stories and plays for BBC Radio 4.

Karen Mann
Fisher

Trained at the Royal Scottish Academy of Music and Drama, Karen has worked in many of the major Repertory Theatres including the Glasgow Citizens', West Yorkshire Playhouse and Birmingham Rep. Much of Karen's work has been as an actor-musician at the Watermill Theatre, Newbury, in award winning productions such as *Fiddler on the Roof, The Gondoliers* and *Sweeney Todd*, playing the part of Mrs Lovett which transferred to London's West End. She has also appeared in several productions of *Return to the Forbidden Planet* playing the part of Gloria (West End, Japan, 1995 British Tour). TV includes *My Family* (BBC) and *Death of a Salesman* (STV). She is delighted to be working with Kali again after being part of the initial production of *Another Paradise* (2008 Edinburgh Festival).

Sarah Paul
Lisa, Michelle, Thomas Paine

Trained at the Central School of Speech and Drama. Theatre includes *Triumph of Love* and *Antony & Cleopatra* (Manchester Royal Exchange); *'Tis Pity She's A Whore* (Southwark Playhouse); *Celestina* (Birmingham Rep); *One Minute* (Sheffield Crucible/Bush Theatre); *Who's Harry* (Pleasance

Theatre); *Pergolesi* (Arcola Theatre) and Chet Baker's *Speedball*. TV: *Man Stroke Woman* (Series 1 & 2); *Holby City*; *Murphy's Law*; *The Catherine Tate Show*; *EastEnders*; *Doctors*; *Silent Witness*; *Casualty* and *Judge John Deed* (BBC); *The IT Crowd* (Channel 4); *Recovery*; *The Bill* and *Ultimate Force* (ITV). Film: *Call of the Hunter*, *What Am I?* and *Faking It*. Radio: *A Surfeit of Lampreys*, *Persephone*, *Soldier Boy*, *Les Miserables* (BBC Radio 4). Sarah received the BBC Radio Drama Carleton Hobbs Award.

Richard Rees
Marcus

Theatre: *For King and Country* (Drayton Arms); *Cinderella, Twelfth Night, Tears of the Indians* (Southampton Nuffield); *Three Sisters, The Queen of Spades and I* (Orange Tree); *M Butterfly* (Shaftesbury); *The Taming of the Shrew, Antony and Cleopatra* (Haymarket); *A Midsummer Night's Dream, Bashville* (Open Air Theatre); *The White Devil, The Way of the World, The Seagull* (Glasgow Citizens); *Romeo and Juliet* (Deptford Albany Empire) and Kali's initial production of *Another Paradise* (2008 Edinburgh Festival). Film and TV: *Survivors, Torn, The Omen, Do Not Be Afraid, Pinochet In Suburbia, In the Beginning, Death On Everest, The Healer*.

Chand Martinez
Enoch

Film includes *Billy Bonfire* (GC films) and *Nadine* (Matchstix Productions). Theatre: *Agreste* (Dende Collective/ Lyric Hammersmith); *The Alchemist* (Cornish Theatre Collective); *The Marriage of Figaro* (Tara Arts); *Romeo and Juliet* (YSC); *Dark River* (Big Picture Company); *Wise Guys* (Theatre Centre) and Kali's initial production of *Another Paradise* (Edinburgh Festival 2008). He created the dance/physical precision character, *The War* with director Liam Steel for Theatre Centre's

controversial production, *Devotion*. A RADA graduate, he also trained at the BBC, London Mime School and Little Angel Puppet Theatre. He constructed and operated puppets for *Story Makers* (CITV), *Adventures of Baron Munchhausen* (Southwark Playhouse) and *Jelly Bean Jack* and *The Sorcerers Apprentice* (Little Angel Theatre).

Janet Steel
Director

Artistic Director of Kali since 2003, Janet began her career as an actress. Theatre: *Cinders, A Colder Climate* (Royal Court Theatre), *Blood Wedding* (Half Moon), *Romeo and Juliet* (Sherman & Albany), *Oedipus Rex* (Tara Arts). TV: *An English Christmas, The Bride, Gems, The Refuge, Shalom Salaam*. Janet began directing in 1988 as assistant to Tessa Schneideman at Loose Change Theatre, where she directed her first full-length piece, *White Biting Dog*. Directing: *Behzti* (Birmingham Rep), *April in Paris, Bretevski Street, A Hard Rain, Top Girls* (Northampton Royal), *Exodus* (Belgrade Coventry); *Antigone, The Mother, Orpheus Descending, An Ideal Husband, Romeo and Juliet, The Knockey, Serious Money* (Rose Bruford). For Kali: *Sock 'em With Honey, Calcutta Kosher, Chaos, Paper Thin, Deadeye, Zameen* and Kali's initial production of *Another Paradise* at the 2008 Edinburgh Festival.

Alice Hoult
Set & Costume Designer

Born and bred in Manchester, Alice trained in Design for Performance at Central Saint Martins, London, graduating with a first in 2004. Recent work: Set and costume design for *Another Paradise* (Kali, Edinburgh Festival 2008); Assistant Designer for *The Dying of Today* (Arcola Theatre, 2008); Costume design for *Playing God* (Deafinitely Theatre, Soho Theatre, 2007); *Drink Me* (Pins and Needles Dance Company, Isle of Wight, 2007); set and costume designs for Shakespeare seasons at Arts Educational, London, 2006 and 2007. Alice regularly assists a muralist, makes drawings in her studio in and has a secret life as a cheesemonger.

Eva Auster
Video Designer

BA(Hons) in Drama and Theatre Studies and an MA in Advanced Theatre Practice at Central School of Speech and Drama. Credits include: Animation Artist, *The Last Round*, 2004; Media Designer, *Romeo & Juliet*, 2005; Co-director, Jez Butterworth's *The Night Heron*, 2005; Media Assistant, MiE, 2006; Visual Media Designer, *8 People 8 Days 8 Mins...* 2008; Visual Media Designer, *Saturated Pegbox – A Play*, 2008; Projection Designer and Co-director, *Derive*, 2008 (Stay Tuned Festival '08); Visual Director, *On the Face of It*, 2008 (Sprint Festival '08); Projection Operator, *What If...?* 2008 (Shunt); Video Editor, *Huis Clos Tango*, 2008; Projection Designer, STILL II, 2008 (Syndromus Theatre, International Workshop Festival); Visual Media Designer, STILL III, 2008 (Syndromus Theatre, Fair of Culture Festival 08, Zagreb). Video Artist, *Where's My Desi Soulmate?* 2009 (Rifco Arts).

Beth Hoare-Barnes
Company Stage Manager

Beth spent much of last year with Fevered Sleep, on *Brilliant and An Infinite Line*, both devised installation-based pieces about light. Previously Beth has stage managed *Duck!* (Unicorn Theatre), a one-man show by Jack Thorne (Arcola) and an outdoor promenade performance with London Bubble. Beth has spent a summer at Regent's Park Open Air Theatre and has toured nationally with Watford Palace, Graeae, Theatre-Rites, Theatre Centre and Wildcard. She spent four years in the US studying and working as a Stage Manager and Lighting Designer, where

she received an MFA and designed professionally in New York, Cleveland and Columbus.

Jessica Thanki
Assistant Director & Assistant Stage Manager

Jessica graduated last year with a 2:1 BA Honours in Theatre Production from London South Bank University. Whilst doing her degree she worked on many shows as an ASM. Jessica also did a three month placement in New York in 2007 at The Thirteenth Street Repertory Theatre in Manhattan where she was a Literary Manager's Assistant. Since graduating Jessica has worked as an ASM on the panto at The West Wing in Slough and on Kali's initial production of *Another Paradise* at the 2008 Edinburgh Festival. Jessica's interests lie in new writing and she hopes to write and direct more in the future.

Sonam Nagewadia
Rehearsal Assistant Stage Manager

Sonam is currently in her final year of training at the Central School of Speech and Drama on the BA Theatre Practice course. Whilst there, she has worked on a range of productions from installations to musicals, including The *Voysey Inheritance*, *A Common Chorus*, *Company*, *Chips with Everything*, *The Visit*, *The Sightless*, and *Interior*. Previously she worked with Harrow Youth Theatre on *A Midsummer Night's Dream*.

Christopher Corner
General Manager

A freelance Theatre Project Manager and Administrator, specialising in new writing, including work with Foco Novo, Joint Stock, Bristol Express, Paines Plough, Half Moon, Royal Court, Moving Theatre, The Wedding Collective, Lifeblood Theatre Co, Scott Davison Productions, Andy Jordan Productions and The Wrestling School.

ANOTHER PARADISE

First published in 2009 by Oberon Books Ltd
521 Caledonian Road, London N7 9RH
Tel: 020 7607 3637 / Fax: 020 7607 3629
e-mail: info@oberonbooks.com
www.oberonbooks.com

A catalogue record for this book is available from the British Library.

ISBN: 978-1-84002-920-8

Cover photograph by Robert Workman

Printed in Great Britain by CPI Antony Rowe, Chippenham.

Characters

LISA GRUNDY

27, Smart, office type, trendy glasses, hair tied
up, kind, conscientious. Works in customer
services at the Alien Registration Office. She
has two other identities: MICHELLE BOHEME,
a biker who wears a leather jacket and has
loose tousled hair, a bit of a Lara Croft. She
has a laconic but direct street quality. She
appears unconcerned and casual, matter of fact,
nonchalant, chews gum. THOMAS PAINE, a
human rights activist who wears a tricorne hat. A
Scarlet Pimpernel type. He is a little outlandish
and speaks passionately, with a flourish, possibly
with a Norfolk/American accent. When Lisa is
being Michelle or Thomas the costume changes
must be simple but effective. Though her other
identities have different energies, being in
different situations, she is still essentially herself.

ENOCH DAWES

30s, Accountant, small, wears glasses,
unremarkable.

ABIGAIL TOMLIN

40s, Loves all creatures, warm, caring, natural.
Works at the Eden bird sanctuary.

MARCUS TOMLIN

Early 50s, Successful businessman, arrogant,
superior, still quite handsome, cowardly. Owns
several companies and a hospital.

CAPTAIN FISHER

52, female. Police Captain specialising in
internal security. Wears a dark uniform and
boots. Strong, determined, meticulous, appears
mean but has a caring side.

Leamington Spa, England.

SETTING

The use of computer/projection screens is necessary in the overall design.

The World of the Card. Represented by music and a projected image of an identity card/electronic circuit board on the back wall with a throbbing pulse running through it. When the characters are being scanned their photo and personal data appear on the screens. The card speaks using a recording of the character's own voice, as if it is part of their being. Any other computer spoken words, ie the security scanner, are in a neutral female voice.

The Tomlin House. This is the main central set, a comfortable, middle class living room but slightly unusual as one side of it is like a Kew gardens tropical hot house, elaborately crowded with exotic plants. This is Abi's indoor garden. On the back wall is a archway out to the front door and next to that bookshelves that reach to the top of the set. There is a bureau where Marcus keeps files and also where the whisky and glasses live. Across the room is the way out to the kitchen. There are three pictures on the wall, Van Gogh's 'The Irises', a Brazilian rainforest bird, and a palmistry etching. Also on the wall there is a biometric reader, it is palm sized and is their security system – used to open the doors or lock up. There is also a CCTV switch and small screen.

The Alien Registration Office. Downstage and to the side of the Tomlin house. Cold and impersonal with a luminescent white wall. Bowl of apples on the desk. A sign on the wall reads 'Alien registration, Customer Services' And on the desk is a name plate, 'Lisa Grundy'.

The Interrogation Room, This area is in front of the Alien Registration desk. It is darker with just a chair.

The Precinct. Downstage, other side of the Tomlin House, it is run down, neglected and has a dilapidated car park sign on the brick wall.

All locations, once established, can incorporate as much of the space as they need. Characters sometimes move between the scenes in view of the audience. Sometimes they watch other scenes.

Where I say 'Reader' it refers to a (portable) biometric identification reading device that accepts cards, fingerprints, palms, iris/retina information.

Act One

SCENE 1

Blackout. On the back of the set a green light throbs, an electrical impulse, like green blood through the circuitry of a large identity card image. An electronic life force getting brighter and stronger.

Music pounds. The characters enter and all face front. In a stylised, choreographed routine they each hold up a palm, offer their fingerprints or open an eye wide to show an iris. Then each in turn offers an ID card to an invisible Biometric Reader. A laser beam scans across it. Pictures of palms, fingerprints or irises will flash up on the computer screens correspondingly. Once the characters have been scanned they leave. As the words flash up on the screen/monitors they are simultaneously spoken by the Card. This applies throughout the play.

LISA is smart, carries briefcase.

'VERIFIED' flashes up on the monitors.

MARCUS is carrying the Financial Times.

'VERIFIED' flashes up on the monitors.

ABI is slightly disorganised. She carries a large shoulder bag with lots of papers sticking out and a bag of groceries. She is searching through her bag for her ID card. Offers her palm.

'ERROR' flashes up on the monitors.

She wipes her hands on her clothes and tries her palm again.

'PLEASE WASH HANDS' flashes up on the monitors.

She shows her iris.

'VERIFIED' flashes up on the monitors.

ABI breathes a sigh of relief and leaves.

FISHER, in police sunglasses, calm, self-assured.

'SPECIAL ACCESS PRIVILEGES' flashes up on the monitors.

She moves off but turns to watch ENOCH.

ENOCH carries a briefcase. The music stops and the sound of a heart beat takes over. Lights focus in on him.

THE CARD: Enoch Dawes. British citizen. Accountant. Last purchase fish and chips for two, Friday. One living parent. No dependents. One wife. Biometric identification… error… Enoch Dawes, Denied. (*ENOCH tries again.*) Enoch Dawes, fish on Fridays. 6 wives. 4 wives. 3 alcoholic chips. Error. Denied.

'ERROR. DENIED.' flashes up on the monitors.

He offers a palm print. The Card is malfunctioning and speech slows. The heart beat stops and an alarm goes off.

'TERMINAL ERROR. IDENTITY VOID. PLEASE SEEK ASSISTANCE.' flashes up on the monitors.

ENOCH is confused. He looks around, embarrassed. Everyone has gone except FISHER on the other side of the stage. They stare at each other. He turns and leaves, as does FISHER.

SCENE 2

The Tomlin house. In the middle of the floor is a pile of clothes, big old trousers still tucked into some wellies, coat, balaclava and a pair of large wire cutters.

MARCUS and MICHELLE enter, they are both wearing black motorcycle helmets with dark visors down. They stand opposite each other. He removes his helmet. She removes hers, throws her head back swishing her tousled hair, like in a shampoo ad. He watches, surprised.

MARCUS: You're a woman.

MICHELLE: Is that a problem?

MARCUS: No. Drink?

MICHELLE: Water.

MARCUS: Water?

MICHELLE: Water.

MARCUS: I'll have to have a look.

He exits to kitchen.

MICHELLE looks around, sees an expensive looking handbag on the chair and goes to it. Pushes her hand deep into it, rummages around, and pulls out a trowel. She puts it back and feels again. She pulls out secateurs. She puts them back and quickly pulls out a long feather. She looks about her. Then her eye catches something near to the bag. An ID card. She picks it up. Holds it up to the light, smells it, bites it, smiles and puts it into her pocket.

She then goes to the security system panel on the wall – a biometric reader. Places her hand on it. A scanner beam passes across her hand, it sounds a 'reject' beep, flashes red and speaks, 'TRY AGAIN'. She steps back and looks at it. She presses some buttons underneath it.

MARCUS: Here you are.

She takes the glass and drinks.

Found some in the tap.

MICHELLE: Where do I powder my nose?

MARCUS: Between your eyes and down a bit.

She waits for a sensible response.

Out there. First on the left.

He indicates the hall. She hands him the glass and exits still holding the feather.

MARCUS sees the pile of clothes and moves them with his foot to see what they are.

ABI enters from the hall wearing cosy pyjamas, slippers and her hair up in a towel. She heads for the pile.

You?

ABI: What?

MARCUS: You're here.

ABI: Of course I'm here.

MARCUS: I thought you were out.

ABI: I was.

MARCUS: Everyone asked after you. I said you were ill.

ABI: I'm not.

MARCUS: I lied.

ABI: You didn't have to.

MARCUS: I couldn't tell them the truth, could I?

ABI: I was working.

She picks up the old coat and gives it a shake. Bird feathers flutter out.

MARCUS: Is that what you call it?

ABI: I left you a message.

MARCUS: You weren't in your office.

ABI: It was an emergency.

MARCUS: Security located your car.

ABI: Pardon?

MARCUS: I thought something might have happened to you.

ABI: You tracked me?

MARCUS: You let me down. You never let me down.

ABI: How dare you?

MICHELLE enters unseen by them. She casually watches.

MARCUS: I was worried. Would you rather I'd called out the police?

ABI: You spied on me?

MARCUS: For your own safety.

ABI: This has nothing to do with my safety.

MARCUS: I know where you were. How could you do this to me?

ABI: It was important.

MARCUS: Nothing's important enough to go to Coventry.

She picks up the wire cutters and heads towards the kitchen.

MARCUS: What are you doing with those?

ABI: Making cocoa.

She exits to the kitchen.

MARCUS: (*Softly to ABI's back.*) Traitor.

Goes to pour himself a whisky and notices MICHELLE.

Great places hospitals. Should have bought more of them while they were going cheap. Never find staff more dedicated than in a hospital. Lovely people. Record profits.

MICHELLE waits. MARCUS remembers ABI and now wants to get MICHELLE out. He puts down the water glass and gets her helmets for her.

Right. Well, thanks for the lift. Great bike. You don't see many Harleys around these days. Used to have one myself. Powerful.

ABI enters with two mugs of cocoa.

Thrilling. I'll tell you something, I haven't had a ride like that in years. Let alone from a woman.

ABI: Cocoa?

MARCUS sees her and is momentarily flustered.

MARCUS: Abi.

ABI: (*To MICHELLE.*) Hello.

MARCUS: This is…er

MICHELLE: Michelle.

MARCUS: She's a…doctor.

MICHELLE: I'm a courier.

> *MARCUS is surprised. MICHELLE flashes her ID card. They both lean in to look. Then she holds out a portable biometric reader to ABI.*

> Sign.

ABI: What for?

MICHELLE: Your husband. You can check he's all there.

> *ABI looks at them both in disbelief. She gives MARCUS his cocoa then suspiciously gives a thumb print. MICHELLE puts her portable Reader away and grabs the helmets. She goes to the door and turns back and smiles briefly at them before leaving.*

> *ABI and MARCUS stare after her.*

ABI: I've never had to sign for you before.

MARCUS: I've never been couriered.

ABI: Where did you find her?

MARCUS: She was in the car park. She offered me a lift.

ABI: And you accepted?

MARCUS: I was locked out of my car.

ABI: Your car doesn't lock you out. It has state of the art biometric recognition. She could be anyone.

MARCUS: It was freezing. If you'd been there you'd know. But you weren't, were you?

ABI: Don't turn this around on me.

MARCUS: You were in Coventry.

ABI: I was at the perimeter, I didn't go in. I wouldn't.

MARCUS: What did you bundle into your car?

ABI: Nothing.

MARCUS: You were seen.

ABI: I wasn't doing anything wrong.

MARCUS: That's not how it looks.

ABI: I was just doing my job.

MARCUS: At night?

ABI: Yes.

MARCUS: What was it?

>*ABI doesn't respond.*

Tell me.

ABI: Stop it.

MARCUS: Tell me.

ABI: Alright! (*Beat.*) It was a bird.

MARCUS: A bird?

ABI: A bird. But not just any bird, an *Arfak Astrapia.* A bird of paradise. Iridescent purple, green and bronze. A long, long broad tail, velvety black breast and a very sexy head plumage.

MARCUS: You've been buying birds from criminals?

ABI: They're not criminals.

MARCUS: What would an Arfak thingy bird of paradise be doing in Coventry? Bird trafficking is illegal.

ABI: I'm not trafficking. It was a rescue. She'd been badly treated. I couldn't leave her to die.

MARCUS: Yes you could.

ABI: You're a man without feeling.

MARCUS: And you feel for every bloody thing. Get rid of it before anyone finds out.

ABI: I'm not going to turf her out. She's at the Sanctuary and she needs attention. I have to log her and ID her. Everything must be logged and ID'd. She might even be legal. You'd be surprised how many birds have multi citizenship.

MARCUS: You don't know what you're dealing with.

ABI: I'm protecting rare breeds from extinction. Nothing is more important than the natural world.

MARCUS: Tell that to the police when they arrest you.

ABI: Nature teaches us about ourselves. A party of small children came to the Sanctuary yesterday. Some of them had never seen birds so close before. They were so excited, one of the children wandered off and got lost. We found her with the Mongolian swan. Can you imagine losing a child? A small child.

She sits.

I'm sorry, Marcus. I'm sorry.

He gently takes her hand.

MARCUS: Why don't you think about adopting again?

ABI: What?

MARCUS: A child.

ABI: What for?

MARCUS: You're a woman.

ABI: I thought you didn't want one.

MARCUS: We could have Sunday picnics in the park.

ABI: I don't want to adopt.

MARCUS: It'll be good for you.

ABI: We could still have our own children.

MARCUS: It hasn't happened.

ABI: Sex might help.

MARCUS gets up tops up his drink.

MARCUS: I want you to be happy.

ABI: I know.

MARCUS: You're everything to me.

ABI: It all seemed so clear once upon a time. I don't know who I am any more.

MARCUS: Isn't that just one of the beauties of the system? You pop in your card and there you are, perfectly formed and gorgeously catalogued.

ABI: You're not taking me seriously.

MARCUS: I am. You need to get out more, meet some new people, not just birds. Why don't you come to the campaign meeting.

ABI: I don't want to 'Save Leamington Spa'.

MARCUS: Well you should. We're in danger. Isn't that what you do, protect endangered species?

ABI sorts out and picks up the rest of the pile from the floor.

ABI: We are not endangered, we live in the safest society in the civilised world.

MARCUS: I won't feel safe until they've moved Coventry and all its delinquents to some other Godforsaken place. The government should never have sent them to Coventry in the first place.

ABI: It was a barbaric act of inhumanity.

SAYAN KENT

MARCUS: Isle of Man would have been much better. Or Wales. They could have romped around the valleys in blissful ignorance.

ABI: How can you say that?

MARCUS: Coventry's a blight and it's eight miles down the road. It has to go. House prices are dropping in Leamington Spa.

She shakes her head at him in disbelief goes to the security panel on the wall.

A few always have to suffer for the sake of the common good.

ABI: I don't believe that.

MARCUS: You do, that's why you can sleep soundly in your bed at night.

ABI: (*To the Reader.*) Lock.

The Reader sounds an 'accept' beep, flashes green and speaks, 'LOCK'.

I'm going to bed.

She goes. MARCUS checks his watch then finishes his drink. He checks the hall to make sure ABI's gone. Then whispers to the security Reader.

MARCUS: Open.

The Reader sounds an 'accept' beep, flashes green and speaks, 'OPEN'.

Ssh.

He tiptoes out.

SCENE 3

The Card image pulsates. Heartbeat/music. ABI enters. The other characters watch her from wherever they are. The voice of the card speaks the words.

ABI shows her iris.

'ERROR.' flashes up on the monitors.

She tuts, sticks out her tongue.

'PLEASE INSERT CARD.' flashes up on the monitors.

ABI rummages through her bag to find her card. She thinks, then takes off a shoe and holds the sole of her bare foot to be scanned.

'VERIFIED' flashes up on the monitors.

ABI sighs relief. Lights down and up brightly on the next scene.

SCENE 4

The Alien Registration Office. LISA has a laptop computer on her desk. She types intermittently throughout. ENOCH stands against a wall, uncomfortable and out of place. He is scared. Less-tidy looking than he was in the beginning. She is sympathetic to him.

ENOCH: It's very unusual.

LISA: Unusual. (*Types.*)

ENOCH: Unfamiliar. Never happened before

LISA: What is usual?

ENOCH: I wake up. Next to my wife. Breakfast. Go to work. Come home. Supper. Go to bed. That's usual. For me.

LISA: I'm Lisa Grundy, I'll be handling your case. We don't know who you are, Mr 41190875/UP366.

ENOCH looks up to the Alien Registration sign on the wall.

ENOCH: I'm not an alien. I've never been an alien.

LISA: Don't worry.

ENOCH: I'm Enoch Dawes. Accountant. Manfred Gavril Chartered Accountants. I have plenty of money and a beautiful wife, Angelica.

LISA: Angelica.

ENOCH: She's a model.

LISA: Where did you meet?

ENOCH: In a cinema queue, *It's A Wonderful Life*.

LISA: Is it?

ENOCH: Not today.

LISA types.

I took the train from London. Paid cash. I shouldn't be here. They said I should come though. I don't know what to do. It's all gone.

LISA: It is unusual.

ENOCH: Vanished. Into thin air. Vamoosh.

LISA: But you're still here.

ENOCH: A technicality.

LISA: Is that what they told you?

ENOCH: Pinch me.

LISA: I'm not allowed.

ENOCH: Go on, pinch me, touch me.

LISA: I can't.

ENOCH: Feel my hand. It's real.

LISA: I believe you.

ENOCH: No you don't.

LISA: I do.

ENOCH: They didn't.

LISA: Did they pinch you?

ENOCH: They weren't allowed.

LISA: It's standard procedure. We're not allowed to touch.

ENOCH: But I want you to. I'm human. Can I touch you?

LISA: No. The alarms will go off.

ENOCH: Are you alarmed?

LISA: Do I look it?

ENOCH: You have a pinkishness in your cheeks. That could suggest alarm.

LISA: Well I'm not. You're just not allowed to touch me. It's for our protection.

ENOCH: I only asked.

LISA: It's an unusual request. (*Types.*)

ENOCH: Unusual day. (*He watches her.*) You think I'm making this all up? You're just like them. I had a life, I don't now.

LISA: Do you find that you are a black and white person? Clarity. Polarity. Contrast. Definitives.

ENOCH: Clarity?

LISA: As opposed to subtle, nebulous, fluid, ambidextrous.

ENOCH: Ambidextrous?

LISA: Yes or no?

ENOCH: Like you're a somebody and I'm a nobody?

She observes him then types.

LISA: What colour is your tie?

ENOCH: Green.

LISA: Blue?

ENOCH: No.

LISA: A bit yellowish?

ENOCH: It's green.

LISA: Just green?

ENOCH: Absolutely.

LISA: Not even a hint of black?

ENOCH: I don't know what this has got to do with me.

LISA: It's your tie.

ENOCH: I don't care about the tie.

LISA: I do.

ENOCH: Call it what you like. Red, if you want.

LISA: Red it is then.

ENOCH: But it's not red.

LISA: Yes it is.

ENOCH: It's green.

LISA: No.

ENOCH: Really.

LISA: We agreed. Red.

ENOCH: You did.

LISA: You suggested red.

ENOCH: Only because it doesn't matter. It's just a tie.

LISA: Then it's red.

ENOCH: Okay it's red.

LISA: Good. (*Types.*)

ENOCH: (*Pause, then quietly.*) But it's really green.

LISA: Anything else you want to add, before you leave?

ENOCH: Is this it? I haven't told you anything.

LISA: You've told me lots.

ENOCH: Where am I supposed to go?

LISA: You should see it as stepping out for a short break.

ENOCH: I've heard about people like me. They get on a train and disappear. Suddenly. No one hears of them again. And they end up in a place that no one leaves. It's like a prison but worse.

LISA: Even prisons let people out eventually.

ENOCH: There's crime in this place and aliens, non people. There's danger, rife cannibalism.

LISA: I've never heard of such a place.

ENOCH: (*Quietly.*) Coventry.

LISA: Do you believe in fairy tales?

ENOCH: No but I'm scared of cannibals.

LISA: Relax.

ENOCH: I can't go anywhere, I can't do anything. I can't even work. Last week I was watching television with Angelica. On the settee. It's blue. Just blue. Everything was so simple then. Now I can't get into the flats. The scanner doesn't recognise me and no one answers the doors. I've left her notes. I waited for her at Luigi's, our favourite diner. But she never turned up.

LISA: (*Concerned.*) Angelica isn't married to you anymore.

ENOCH: She is. You're trying to confuse me. You've messed up my life and now you want to send me to Coventry.

LISA: I don't. You're free to go. You'll be hearing from the department in due course.

ENOCH: I haven't got a anywhere to go.

LISA: (*Exasperated.*) Then try Coventry. It's a cash economy. No questions and no cannibalism.

ENOCH: I won't desert my wife.

LISA: You don't have a wife. Currently you don't have an identity.

ENOCH: I'm Enoch Dawes.

LISA: That's just a name. At present none of your biometric information matches any of our records.

ENOCH: (*Desperate.*) I don't understand.

LISA: Think of your ID card as the portal to your digital soul. It links you to who you are. As long as you are attached to a corresponding file on the database the card could say you were a mouse and I would believe it. Even if you didn't look like a mouse. Which you do, slightly. Even if you stood in front of me as you are and your data told me you were Monty the Mouse I would accept that as true. I would greet you as Monty and offer you a piece of cheese.

ENOCH: I'm not a mouse.

LISA: It was an example.

ENOCH: Do I sound like a mouse?

LISA: Not really.

ENOCH: I am a mouse.

LISA: You're not a mouse.

ENOCH: How do you know?

LISA: (*Smiles, pause.*) I've registered your claim for citizenship.

ENOCH: I'm already a citizen.

LISA: Stay out of trouble and don't try and go anywhere where you need to be scanned or you'll be arrested.

ENOCH: What makes a man a criminal?

LISA: A green tie.

He looks at his tie.

What colour is your tie?

ENOCH: (*Pause.*) Red.

She smiles at him then goes back to her typing. He looks puzzled and rather like a frightened animal.

SCENE 5

The Tomlin house. Morning. ABI is polishing the leaves on her plants and stroking them with loving care. She wears a pinny and scarf around her hair. An attractive housewife image. She talks to her plants.

ABI: You haven't seen my card, have you? No, of course you haven't. You don't have eyes. You, you just sit and be. Just to be. Spreading your fronds... I'm not worried about it either. Yes, I know it's just a piece of plastic and not very environmentally friendly...

Doorbell rings. ABI sighs. The CCTV screen on the security panel shows MICHELLE at the door. She holds up her ID card.

We never get enough quality time together.

ABI goes to the security system panel on the wall Places her hand on it. A scanner beam passes across her hand, it sounds an 'accept' beep, flashes green and speaks, 'OPEN'. MICHELLE's image disappears.

MICHELLE enters with a cardboard box.

I remember you.

MICHELLE hands the box to ABI and gets out her portable Reader for a signature. Though she is also preoccupied, looking around the floor area for something.

MICHELLE: Sign.

ABI checks the box first. She opens it and stares. Catches her breath.

ABI: Oh, oh, she's beautiful.

ABI gives MICHELLE a thumb print. MICHELLE looks at her Reader and presses some buttons on it. Smiles to ABI. She doesn't move to go but shiftily starts looking at the floor as if she's dropped something.

Is there anything else?

MICHELLE: I lost something. The night I delivered your husband. A small identity bracelet.

ABI: Was it silver?

MICHELLE: Yes

ABI: I wondered if it was yours.

She goes to get it from a drawer.

I found it in my handbag. I don't know how it could have got there. I presume Marcus dropped it in, thinking it was mine.(*Looks at it.*) It's very pretty. ELF. Is that you? What does it stand for?

MICHELLE: Equality, liberty, fraternity.

ABI: Oh. Well, here you are. The catch needs fixing.

ABI hands her the delicate bracelet.

MICHELLE: Thanks.

MICHELLE looks at the catch, fiddles with it and then puts it on her wrist.

ABI: Do you like plants?

MICHELLE: Not really.

ABI: I have to be surrounded by nature.

MICHELLE: You should travel the world.

ABI: And do what?

MICHELLE: See nature.

ABI: I see nature everywhere. A dandelion between the paving stones, an ant under the sink. And there are still some lovely hedges outside.

MICHELLE: You like birds.

MICHELLE points to the picture on the wall.

ABI: I love birds, rainforest birds especially. Perhaps because I've never seen them. Not in their own habitat and there's hardly any rainforest left now. I travelled a bit when I was younger. Before I married. When it was just me. It was good then. Have you travelled?

MICHELLE: It's my job.

ABI: I mean far afield.

MICHELLE: Go anywhere on a bike.

ABI: That must be liberating.

MICHELLE: I'm single.

ABI: Just go when you feel like it.

MICHELLE: Easy.

ABI: Wherever you want.

MICHELLE: Across continents.

ABI: Seas.

MICHELLE: Mountains.

ABI: Skies.

MICHELLE: Free.

ABI: Like a bird.

MARCUS enters, sees MICHELLE. She offers her ID card. He glances at it.

MARCUS: Ah, the courier.

MICHELLE takes a book out of her jacket and hands it to MARCUS.

MICHELLE: Sign.

MARCUS gives her a thumb print. ABI guides MICHELLE out.

ABI: Thank you. Let me know if there's…anything else.

ABI and MICHELLE exit towards front door.

MARCUS: *The Rights of Man?*

MARCUS is puzzled, puts the books down then he notices the box, checking behind him that ABI is still out of the room, he peeps in. He doesn't see anything at first and then he does and freezes on the spot. Barely able to get a word out.

MARCUS: Sn…Sn…Sn…sn…Sn…Sn…

ABI enters and goes back to her plants.

ABI: It's alright, she won't hurt you.

MARCUS: Snay… snay….

ABI: You're perfectly safe. She's not dangerous. She's for the sanctuary.

MARCUS: Snaayy… sn… sn…

ABI goes over to him and slaps his face.

MARCUS: Ow.

He comes out of his panic-induced stupor and moves to a safer distance.

MARCUS: There's a snake in that box.

ABI: I know.

Picking the box up, lovingly.

MARCUS: What's it doing here?

ABI: She's just been delivered. I'm taking her to the sanctuary just as soon as I find my helmet.

MARCUS: Helmet?

ABI: Motorbike.

MARCUS: You haven't got a helmet.

ABI: No

MARCUS: Or a motorbike.

ABI: I meant handbag.

MARCUS: It's a snake. You work at a bird sanctuary.

ABI: We're opening an animal section.

MARCUS: Really?

ABI: Temporarily.

MARCUS: (*Suspicious.*) Where's it from?

ABI: I don't know yet. She needs to be logged and ID'd.

MARCUS: You didn't buy it? (*Realising.*) You said you wouldn't do this anymore.

ABI: I said no more birds.

MARCUS: It's wrong.

ABI: And you've never done anything wrong.

MARCUS: I'm not the one who's going to get caught.

ABI: Of course not. Have you seen my ID card? I reported it missing this morning.

MARCUS opens his laptop. ABI puts the snake down while looking for her handbag.

MARCUS: You don't look after it properly.

ABI: Do I do anything right? It's my ID. It's no use to anyone else.

MARCUS: It could end up in the wrong hands.

ABI: These aren't like the old cards. These are Unity cards. Impenetrable. Safe as houses. That's what you tell us and your company makes them.

She looks over his shoulder reading the laptop screen.

MARCUS: You still have to be careful.

ABI: That must be a mistake. Who's M. Plum?

MARCUS: Don't do that. It's rude.

ABI: There's a large payment been made to an M. Plum. I don't know any plums. Do you?

MARCUS: I er….

ABI: I'll report it straight-away. Bank security isn't what it used to be. If they lose our money who knows what they'll lose next.

MARCUS: (*Clutching at straws.*) It's the plumbers. I remember authorising it.

ABI: That's a lot of plumbers.

MARCUS: It's was a lot of work.

ABI: What was wrong?

MARCUS: The plumbing.

ABI: Is it fixed?

MARCUS: Yes.

ABI: They're very discreet.

MARCUS: They come when you're out. So as not to disturb you.

Doorbell rings. CCTV shows FISHER waiting outside the door. She looks to the camera, smiles and shows her ID.

ABI: (*Worried.*) It's the police. You don't think... (*She glances over to the snake box.*)

MARCUS: I'll deal with her.

ABI: Open.

The wall reader flashes red, sounds a reject beep and speaks 'TRY AGAIN'.

Open.

The wall reader flashes red, sounds a reject beep and speaks 'TRY AGAIN'. ABI walks up to it and places her hand on it but it rejects her again, 'TRY AGAIN'.

MARCUS: (*To the Reader.*) Open.

It flashes green, sounds an 'accept' beep and speaks 'OPEN'. The CCTV goes off as FISHER leaves the picture.

ABI: It worked perfectly just now.

MARCUS re-programmes the buttons on the panel.

MARCUS: Now try.

ABI tries again and it rejects her, 'TRY AGAIN'. FISHER enters and watches them. She notices the snake box and has a peek in.

ABI: Another piece of useless technology.

MARCUS: There's nothing wrong with the technology.

FISHER: Sometimes if you give these things a thump they reset themselves.

MARCUS gives a broad false smile to FISHER.

MARCUS: (*Testy.*) There's nothing wrong with the technology.

ABI picks up the snake box and leaves the room, wanting to get it away from FISHER.

FISHER: I won't waste your time Mr Tomlin, I want you to stop the 'Save Leamington Spa' campaign.

MARCUS: Impossible.

FISHER: I know you don't like Coventry being where it is, love, but on the whole we manage it very nicely. Rousing local support to get Coventry moved is tantamount to inciting violence. That's not allowed.

MARCUS: You pander to those reprobates. What about the lawful citizen?

FISHER: I'm asking for your co-operation. I don't want you or anyone else to get hurt.

MARCUS: It's your job to protect me. I take it you know your job.

FISHER: I'm negotiating preventative measures.

MARCUS: I will not curb my freedom of speech just to make your life easier. This is still a free country.

FISHER: (*Amused.*) Don't be silly.

MARCUS: There's vandalism, burglaries, kidnappings. You know it's them.

FISHER: We're doing our best.

MARCUS: Come off it Fisher, there are cameras everywhere.

FISHER: We can't identify them. They don't have identities.

MARCUS: You should keep them locked up. There are holes in the perimeter fence.

FISHER: We're over budget already.

MARCUS: You're bloody useless.

FISHER picks up The Rights of Man. *Flicks it open and reads the inside cover.*

FISHER: *The Rights Of Man* by Thomas Paine. You surprise me, Mr Tomlin.

MARCUS: It's junk mail.

FISHER: Tom Paine only ever sends his book to accomplices, conspirators or enemies. Which one are you?

MARCUS: I've never even heard of him.

FISHER: Never heard of Thomas Paine? The Age of Reason?

MARCUS: No

FISHER: The Enlightenment?

MARCUS: No

FISHER: The American War of Independence?

MARCUS: That was hundreds of years ago.

FISHER: The French Revolution?

MARCUS: Get to the point Fisher.

FISHER: He was behind them all. (*Looks on the back cover.*) Born 1737, the most influential free thinker of his time, lapsed Quaker and corset maker. Expert at revolutions and writing very long arguments.(*Points to the book.*) Civil Rights activist and revolutionary with knobs on, hounded out of England, imprisoned in France, lived a long time in America.

MARCUS: How can a dead man send me a book?

FISHER: Oh no Mr Tomlin, Thomas Paine is very much alive. And more importantly, Thomas Paine is the unofficial spokesperson for the indigent poor and disenfranchised of Coventry.

Pause. She squints at him, he squints back at her. An understanding passes between them.

MARCUS: Is he, indeed?

FISHER: But he's a slippery fish. I've yet to meet him in the flesh.

MARCUS: I see

FISHER flicks to the front inside cover.

MARCUS: Well, the book is nothing to do with me.

FISHER: Odd. It has your name in it. (*Reads.*) 'My dear Mr Tomlin, it has come to my attention that one of your former enterprises, Uriel Components plc, was the company responsible for updating the identity programme twenty four years ago, which caused the system crash now known Blackout Tuesday.'

MARCUS: Uriel Components did not cause a system crash.

FISHER: (*Continues.*) 'I realise that you were tried and cleared for your part in this vile and unnatural human catastrophe.'

MARCUS: It never even got to court. There was no evidence.

FISHER: 'And I have no wish to rekindle this unpleasant feature of your past. But, kind sir, on behalf of the non-citizens of Coventry I ask that you grant me access to your hospital archives so that I may, in good faith, clear your name once and for all.'

MARCUS: Clear my name?

FISHER: Hospital archives? (*Continues to read.*) 'I will contact you again shortly to arrange a time for us to meet. I have sent you my book as you may not have read it. Yours cordially, Tom.'

MARCUS: Let me see that. (*Takes the book.*)

FISHER: I didn't know you had contact with a self-declared enemy of the State.

MARCUS: This could be anyone.

FISHER: Let's do each other a favour, you scratch my back, I'll scratch yours.

MARCUS: I don't want to scratch anything of yours.

FISHER: Put it this way, you are now linked to a subversive radical extremist. (*Holds the book up.*) That won't look good on your record.

MARCUS: I am not linked to anyone.

FISHER: Then why is this elusive fanatic willing to reveal himself to just visit your dusty archives?

MARCUS: I don't know, he's a blackmailer trying to get information.

FISHER: On what?

MARCUS: The sale of information is worth millions. I get these sorts of letters all the time.

FISHER: From Tom Paine?

MARCUS: From Tom, Dick and Harry.

FISHER: (*Calmly.*) I've never heard of Dick or Harry, only Tom.

She studies him.

I know a lot about you.

MARCUS: So does everyone. I'm a public figure.

FISHER: (*Quietly.*) I know where you go after your bedtime cocoa.

MARCUS: (*Beat.*) You have a funny way of going about things, Captain Fisher.

FISHER: So do you Mr Tomlin. Public archives should be in the records office.

MARCUS: Anything in my hospital is my property. Data Protection.

FISHER: Data Protection. I'm curious. What made you buy that hospital all those years ago? Your job was technology.

MARCUS: I'm a businessman. It was cheap and on the verge of bankruptcy. I've built it into a world class centre of excellence.

FISHER: That's right, the Old Milton General fell into disrepute after Blackout Tuesday when all those patients disappeared.

MARCUS: No one disappeared.

FISHER: What happened to the patients in your hospital on Blackout Tuesday?

MARCUS: It wasn't my hospital then.

FISHER: It was your system blackout. I remember it well. A call came in to the station, nine am, I worked in the canteen in those days. Best breakfasts in the region. But not that morning. The networks were down. State security was on high alert. Prison gates were open and there was widespread identity failure.

MARCUS: Nothing to do with me, I'm afraid.

FISHER: So if you've got any records in your hospital that date back to then I'd like to see them. All information dating back to that day is the property of the state.

MARCUS: Don't try and investigate me, you'll regret it.

FISHER: I know people who are still searching for loved ones.

MARCUS: You're a public servant. The government doesn't look kindly on those who betray its trust.

FISHER: Are you threatening me?

MARCUS: I know where my loyalties lie.

FISHER: I know people whose identities disappeared on that day. Twenty four years ago. Patients who were never returned to their families.

MARCUS: (*Frustrated.*) No one lost their identity and generous compensation was paid for any inconvenience caused.

FISHER: (*A sudden flash of passion.*) What's compensation? How do you compensate a mother losing her child?

Pause. They both take it in.

MARCUS: You've spent too long in Coventry, Fisher, you're going native. If you can't do your job effectively, in an unbiased fashion, I'll happily help you find a less challenging position. Back in the police canteen.

FISHER: You're wrong about information, Mr Tomlin, it's not worth millions, it's priceless.

MARCUS grabs his jacket and laptop leaves in a temper. FISHER thumbs through The Rights of Man. *ABI enters, doesn't notice FISHER. She has her coat on and carries the snake box, surreptitiously.*

Mrs Tomlin.

ABI is caught by surprise, jumps.

You have a snake in the box. Is it a pet?

ABI: No.

FISHER: Is it resident here?

ABI: I'm taking her to the sanctuary.

FISHER: The birds won't like that. Licence?

ABI: Not yet.

FISHER: No licence. Dangerous, foreign, limbless, scaly carnivorous, reptile. I'll have to confiscate it.

ABI: Please. She needs proper care.

FISHER: I'm not going to torture and interrogate it. I don't suppose it could tell me much. Or could it?

They both look at the box. Then at each other.

ABI: She's harmless.

FISHER: Where d'you get it? What exactly are you dealing in?

ABI: I'm not dealing in anything. I love nature.

FISHER: D'you take your clothes off and run around in the buff?

ABI: Sometimes.

FISHER: Thought so.

She gets out her portable Reader to enter details.

Snake. Name? Name?

ABI: Abigail Tomlin.

FISHER: I want the snake's name.

ABI: She doesn't have one.

FISHER: Snake, we'll fill in the rest at the station.

ABI: (*Getting distressed.*) Please. She's distressed.

FISHER: I'll have your details now.

ABI: You know who I am.

FISHER: Just give us your ID then, babe, make it easy.

ABI: Why are you doing this?

FISHER: I have to. Are you hiding something Mrs Tomlin?

ABI: Just enter my name and address. You know it.

FISHER: I can't do that.

ABI: You can do what you like.

FISHER: I wish I could. But I need verification. Or how do I know you are who you say you are.

ABI: You know who I am.

FISHER: Mrs Tomlin, you have to appreciate that I work in a rather grey area where people say all sorts of things. My job is not to take people on their word but on what their card verifies. Verify, to establish the truth, accuracy, reality. *Verificare* from the Latin *verus*, true. That's why I like it. I don't have to make difficult decisions. I can leave that to the judges and politicians.

ABI: Actually I can't find my card at the moment. I've mislaid it.

FISHER: I'll take a thumb print. Plonk it on there for me.

ABI places a thumb on FISHER's Reader .

Ooh dear, where's that been? Give it a wipe.

They try again. FISHER is slightly puzzled. Taps the Reader. Tries her own thumb.

Works for me. (*Holding the reader in front of ABI's iris.*) Keep still. How long have you been calling yourself Mrs Tomlin?

ABI: Since I got married. Fifteen years.

FISHER: You have the most extraordinary eyes.

ABI: In what way?

FISHER: Hidden depths

ABI: I've nothing to hide.

FISHER: (*Looking at her Reader.*) Fascinating.

ABI: What?

FISHER: Nothing. Nothing. Absolutely nothing.

ABI: Meaning?

FISHER: I'm going to have to take you in with your slippery friend.

ABI: What?.

FISHER: My jurisdiction, the unidentified.

ABI: Unidentified? I always have trouble with biometric readers. Even my own security system. Ask my husband.

FISHER: It won't make any difference.

ABI: Are you saying you won't believe either of us?

FISHER: Verificare.

ABI: He's a government advisor.

FISHER: What does that mean? That he's more honest than you? I'm arresting you for possession of an illegal ophidian.

ABI: You can't.

FISHER: I must do my job properly. Mr Tomlin would expect it.

ABI: Mr Tomlin is my husband.

FISHER: Pick up your serpent and save your breath.

ABI: (*Distressed.*) What kind of a world is this?

FISHER: (*Calmly turning on her.*) An accountable one.

SCENE 6

The Precinct. ENOCH clutches a dirty sleeping bag. MARCUS appears the other side of the stage, they look at each other. MARCUS smiles slightly, ENOCH smiles slightly in return. MARCUS leaves. MICHELLE enters. She watches ENOCH for a few moments, he shifts uncomfortably.

MICHELLE: I'm a friend.

ENOCH: I don't have any friends.

MICHELLE: You're new round here, you need friends.

ENOCH: What I'm wondering is, if I'm going to wake up tomorrow and discover I'm a hologram. I mean, as it is I don't exist. Or maybe I'm a decommissioned robot and I'll suddenly realise I'm a small pile of junk circuitry on a scientist's workbench. Tell me I'm part of a huge, mad experiment.

MICHELLE: You're part of a huge, mad experiment.

ENOCH: Who are you?

MARCUS appears on the other side. MICHELLE moves into the shadows.

MARCUS: Hi.

ENOCH: Hi.

MARCUS: Do you want to go for a beer?

ENOCH: I'm not thirsty.

MARCUS: (*Laughs.*) You don't have to drink it.

ENOCH tries to laugh along. He looks around for MICHELLE

ENOCH: I'm with someone.

MARCUS: Right. Another time?

ENOCH: Sure.

MARCUS leaves. MICHELLE appears out of the shadows. Sits on the wall. Eats a stick of gum.

MICHELLE: I've got some news for you. About Angelica.

ENOCH: Angelica? You know her?

MICHELLE: Last night Angelica had dinner in Luigi's.

ENOCH: She went. And I wasn't there.

MICHELLE: She was with her husband, Enoch Dawes.

ENOCH: I'm Enoch Dawes and I wasn't at Luigi's.

MICHELLE: You were Enoch Dawes.

ENOCH: I am Enoch Dawes.

MICHELLE: She was with another man called Enoch Dawes.

ENOCH: Another Enoch Dawes?

MICHELLE: Actually the same but not you. Your identity.
    Another person. Personal data re-appropriation.

ENOCH: Data what?

MICHELLE: He stole your identity.

ENOCH: Stole? My identity has been stolen? That's terrible. I
    have to warn Angelica.

MICHELLE: Angelica knows. He was her lover, now he's
    Enoch Dawes.

ENOCH: No.

MICHELLE: I thought you should know the truth.

ENOCH: I don't want the truth I want my wife. I want my life.
    Exactly as it was.

MICHELLE: It was a lie.

ENOCH: It was mine. She was mine. I'm a wealthy accountant.
    I have a long list of clients waiting for their tax returns.

MICHELLE: You resigned.

ENOCH: No, I didn't.

MICHELLE: You didn't want to be an accountant anymore.
    You're now a fireman.

ENOCH: I'm not big enough to be a fireman.

MICHELLE: You're six foot two. Strong and handsome.

ENOCH: Handsome?

She nods.

The bitch.

MICHELLE: You're a very good fireman.

ENOCH: Am I? Is he? Women prefer firemen. I could become a fireman. Who cares about Enoch Dawes? I want to be a fireman.

MICHELLE: You're too small.

ENOCH: I can have his identity. He became me. I can become him.

MICHELLE: It doesn't work like that.

ENOCH: I've got savings, investments, stocks, how much will I need?

MICHELLE: Stealing specific identities is unpredictable, illegal and very expensive. You don't have a penny. You don't even have a name.

ENOCH: I'm Enoch Dawes.

MICHELLE: If you need somewhere to stay go to Mrs Plum's. She'll give you some cash-in-hand work.

ENOCH: What kind of work?

MICHELLE: Listening, mostly.

ENOCH: Who to?

MICHELLE: People with a lot of money and bad sleeping habits.

ENOCH: Women?

MICHELLE: Men and women.

ENOCH: Men?

MICHELLE: There's a lot of loneliness.

She walks away.

ENOCH: Just a minute, is this tie green or red?

MICHELLE: (*Beat.*) Don't bother wearing one, it doesn't suit you.

SCENE 7

Music. The Card image pulsates. MARCUS enters and holds out his palm to be scanned. Heartbeat.

THE CARD: Marcus Tomlin, Male. Status: Alpha. Credit rating good. One wife. Campaign leader Save Leamington Spa, low risk. Founder of Unity Electronics and Uriel Components. Advisor on key identity technology. VIP special privileges. Ophidiophobia. Reads *Financial Times* and *Men on Men*.

Heart beat stops.

Verified.

MARCUS leaves.

SCENE 8

Alien Registration Office. LISA types notes, intermittently, on her laptop during the interview. There is a bowl of apples, or perhaps just one in its own spotlight.

ABI: Don't think you know me because you know what washing powder I buy, or which TV channels I watch, or how many hotels I've stayed in. It's what that file doesn't tell you that counts. You might know how many lovers I've had but you don't know how much I loved them. You might know which brand of chocolate I buy, but you don't know what I taste when I eat it. You don't know my favourite joke, you don't know what cripples me with laughter and you'll never know which photograph I cry over. You think you know my political persuasions but you don't know what burns inside me, what eats me up, what consumes me with passion, what makes me who I am. You...will never know me.

LISA: Please sit. You'll set the alarms off.

ABI: (*Sits.*) This is unbelievable. That woman arrested me in my own home.

LISA: You were in the house of Marcus and Abigail Tomlin.

ABI: I am Abigail Tomlin.

LISA: (*Beat.*) Not entirely.

ABI: Yes entirely.

LISA: You're divided.

ABI: No, I'm completely certain.

LISA: What I mean is, you might be Mrs, or just Abigail, or purely Tomlin. I'm not sure. But not altogether.

ABI: I know who I am.

LISA: Look at it this way. There are two parts to you. 'A' the biometric you, that is your fingerprints, irises, face, wiggly walk et cetera. And 'B', the file in our system that contains data of you, your prints, irises, face, wiggly walk et cetera. The information of 'A' is processed by a numerical algorithm and entered into the database. The algorithm creates a digital representation of the obtained biometric 'B', you.

ABI: Eh?

LISA: See?

ABI: Just scan me back in.

LISA: I can't do that.

ABI: I want to rejoin my life.

LISA: File.

ABI: File. Life.

LISA: Your file has attached itself to another biometric identity.

ABI: A what?

LISA: Think of yourself in front of a mirror.

ABI: No.

LISA: Another person has your reflection.

ABI: My reflection? Someone else has my reflection?

LISA: It's unusual.

ABI: Wait till my husband hears about this.

LISA: You're married?

ABI: (*Slowly starting to lose it, scary.*) You know I am. Don't play silly tits with me.

LISA: What we have in the system doesn't match what you're saying.

ABI: Biometric Readers often reject me. I'm one of those people who just doesn't get along with technology.

LISA: That's unfortunate.

ABI: I'm a nature person. I like waves on the beach. Singing dolphins.

LISA: In Leamington Spa?

ABI: Do you do this on purpose?

LISA: I'll write 'priority' on your case. I'll also make an application for new citizenship.

ABI: I am a citizen.

LISA: It's faster, safer and currently you're not a citizen. You're in 'transition pending outcome'.

ABI: Don't make me laugh.

LISA: A new identity is clean, unblemished, free of the past, including argumentative siblings and spouses.

ABI: With the total life experience of a new born baby.

LISA: It's becoming a popular choice.

ABI: I'm not going anywhere without my past. Scarred as it is. My…school…my…aunt Jasmine in Broadstairs. My parking offences for God's sake. (*Desperate.*) It's all I've got.

LISA: Things are more fluid than you think.

ABI: Are you trying to brainwash me?

LISA: I'm trying to make it clearer. This morning you were Abigail Tomlin. This afternoon you're not. You can fight it or accept it.

ABI: I'll fight it all the way, I am Abi Tomlin.

LISA: As you wish. (*Types.*)

ABI: Are those apples real?

LISA: Help yourself.

ABI: I'm allergic to apples. Abigail Tomlin is allergic to apples.

LISA: But you're not Abigail Tomlin.

ABI: I'll prove it. But if I die, it'll be your fault.

She picks up an apple and bites. Music. She has another bite. Nothing happens to her. LISA relaxes. ABI mellows.

LISA: It's so much easier to accept it. Go with the flow.

ABI: This is delicious. I haven't had an apple in years. Last time I did I was sick as pig. Thank you.

ABI seems much happier. LISA watches her.

SCENE 9

The Tomlin house. MARCUS is in his shirtsleeves. He has some paperwork in his hand. He is somewhat stressed. FISHER holds a small bunch of freesias.

MARCUS: What were you doing, taking her to the station?

FISHER: It was my duty.

MARCUS: You didn't have to arrest her.

FISHER: I was doing my job effectively in an unbiased fashion.

MARCUS: Don't play games with me.

FISHER: I wouldn't dream of it. (*The flowers.*) These are for Mrs Tomlin. She still throwing up?

MARCUS: Yes.

FISHER: The patter of tiny feet?

MARCUS: No. She ate an apple. She's allergic to apples.

FISHER: What did she eat it for?

MARCUS: I don't know. She wasn't feeling herself.

FISHER: She shouldn't have been sent to registration. Not with you as her husband.

He puts his documents into his case and runs his hands through his hair.

MARCUS: They didn't believe she had a husband. They said she was unidentified. Christ. She's not unidentified. She's my wife not some bloody… The thing is, Fisher, these Unity Cards are good. They are the best. Years of investment has gone into the technology. It's is a new chip, it's hardcore.

FISHER: I'm sorry, sir.

MARCUS: If this gets out it could cut the share value in half. It could ruin me.

FISHER: It's not great for your wife.

MARCUS: These cards are designed to be fraud-proof.

FISHER: You can make an official complaint.

MARCUS: Against my own product? Don't be stupid. I want you to find out what you can, be discreet. This is extremely sensitive. There's someone behind this. I know it. A criminal element. It's not just a simple clerical error.

FISHER: What will you do for me?

MARCUS: Do for you? This doesn't just affect my company, it affects the whole industry, the country. Where's your patriotism?

FISHER: Same place as yours, Mr Tomlin.

They look at each other.

MARCUS: Come to me as soon as you find anything. Only me.

FISHER: Thomas Paine.

MARCUS: What about him?

FISHER: Thomas Paine is bound to know all sorts of criminals…hackers.

MARCUS: So?

FISHER: So, give him the access he requested to your hospital archives and get him on our side. He may be able to help us.

MARCUS: I don't want him on my side, he's a self-declared enemy of the state. Just arrest him and force him to talk.

FISHER: I can't find him. You're the only one who can reel him in. If anyone can find Mrs Tomlin's lost identity he can.

MARCUS: There are no lost identities.

FISHER: Whatever you say.

MARCUS: Don't try and be clever with me.

FISHER: I'm trying to help your wife.

MARCUS: You and I believe in public order. The public needs to know they're safe. And they are because we're talking digital, no one literally evaporates.

FISHER: You're wrong. It destroys lives.

ABI enters in her dressing gown looking the worse for wear. She smiles at them then goes to stroke her plants.

MARCUS: Not mine.

FISHER: Data loss doesn't discriminate. It doesn't make any difference which chips are used in which cards, which system we're running, which firewall is protecting us. Files get corrupted, civil servants mislay data and legal citizens are no longer who they used to be. You or I can't stop it. It's a way of life.

She thrusts the freesias at him and exits. He waves after her.

MARCUS: I'll bear it in mind.

ABI: (*To plants.*) You've missed me. But I'm here now, you can cheer up.

MARCUS composes himself.

MARCUS: You're looking much better.

ABI: I look terrible. Any news?

MARCUS: The snake was deported to Honduras where she had family. Turns out she had legal status.

ABI: Has my new ID card arrived?

MARCUS: Not yet.

ABI: Lost.

MARCUS: It's not lost. It takes time. I'm sorting it out.

ABI: I'm lost. We take so many things for granted.

MARCUS: You're not lost. It's only a card. It's information. It's not real. You're real.

ABI: But I am different.

MARCUS: You've been ill.

ABI: I've been draining away. Through the floor into the earth and mixing with the mud, waiting to be reborn. As a plant, an egg.

MARCUS: It's the apple. You've been hallucinating.

ABI: And now I'm waking up, more awake than I've been before. I look back to the thick cloud I was living in but it's blown away and I can see blue sky, I mean really blue. Bluer than I've ever seen it before and I can smell. Freesias.

MARCUS: Fisher brought you some flowers.

MARCUS gives ABI the freesias.

ABI: It's a new air I'm breathing. I want to live. I didn't know it before. But I know it now. I really want to live.

SCENE 10

Alien Registration Office. ENOCH is standing. His tie is gone. He has an ID card in his hand. He is agitated, angry. LISA is slightly uncomfortable with him being there.

LISA: I'm glad your new card arrived so quickly. Usually it takes much longer. You don't have to come here anymore.

ENOCH: I stole a map.

LISA: I don't need to know that.

ENOCH: Coventry isn't on it. It's just a blur, an MOD restricted area. Look. (*Thrusts a map at her.*) No Coventry. You told me it existed.

LISA: Coventry?

ENOCH: A cash economy no questions and no cannibalism.

LISA: A state of mind.

ENOCH: So I went to the blur.

LISA: It's just a saying, being sent to Coventry.

ENOCH: I've been to Coventry.

LISA: Where everyone ignores you. No one speaks to you.

ENOCH: People spoke to me.

LISA: And now you're a citizen again. You've come back from Coventry, so to speak.

ENOCH: Why is it a blur? Tell me.

LISA: It doesn't exist.

ENOCH: Coventry does exist. It's real. What are you hiding?

LISA: Calm down.

ENOCH: What has this country done? What's happening to people?

Silence.

LISA: When the biometric identity scheme phase 3 was instigated, the whole population was finally put onto the national database. But there were many people living in this country who didn't fulfil the exacting requirements of citizenship. So the government, having invested billions in the program, requisitioned a small city in the Midlands to dump the leftovers in. Coventry, a haven for aliens.

ENOCH: They just left them there?

LISA: Up the creek without a paddle.

ENOCH: No communication with the outside world.

LISA: It's shielded. A measure of containment.

ENOCH: And no one has to prove who they are, just names.

LISA: Just names, can you imagine?

ENOCH: Nothing but a blur.

LISA: It's a little Pandemonium in our Garden of Paradise. Every sovereign state has its Coventry. It's the price we pay for freedom.

ENOCH: (*Holding up his card.*) This isn't freedom.

LISA: Being on the outside can change you. Try to forget it.

ENOCH: (*Hands her his new ID card.*) I don't want it. I don't want to be part of this delusion.

LISA: You've been without your ID for a very short time. You have no idea what it's like to spend your whole life as an outcast.

ENOCH: It isn't mine. I purchased it. Illegally.

LISA: (*Takes this in.*) I see.

LISA puts the card into the terminal. ENOCH gives a thumb print.

ENOCH: I was confused. I thought it would solve everything. But this was a mistake. I don't want to hurt anyone.

LISA presses some keys then smiles relief. A piece of paper comes out of the printer.

LISA: How much did you pay?

ENOCH: Not enough, obviously.

LISA: Oh, good. It's legal. For a minute I thought there was a problem.

ENOCH: There is a problem, it's not me.

LISA: It absolutely is you.

ENOCH: I can't be that person.

LISA: What did you expect?

ENOCH: My own identity back. Or at least the fireman's. My wife likes firemen.

LISA: Did you get married?

ENOCH: Forget it, I'm moving to Coventry.

LISA: Look, this is a good ID. You'll love it. Once you get used to it. Now go home. (*Hands him the printout.*) There's your new address. Bank details. Potted history, employment record. National insurance number. Date of birth. All sorts of interesting things.

ENOCH: I can't just walk into another life.

LISA: This is you now.

ENOCH: Look at it. No one will believe me.

LISA: Of course they'll believe you.

ENOCH: But I've stolen somebody.

LISA: You can't do anything about it now. Cheer up. It could have been a lot worse. I'm glad it's all worked out. Enjoy your new life, Mrs Abigail Tomlin. Abi.

ENOCH looks at her, uncertain.

Lights down.

End of Act One. Interval, if required.

Act Two

SCENE 11

The Card image pulsates. Music. The characters go through the same stylised routines as they did in scene one except for ABI who is in position for the next scene. They offer their cards to be scanned.

'VERIFIED' flashes up on the monitors three times for each of them.

They peel away leaving FISHER alone. Music stops, heart beat. Lights focus in on FISHER.

THE CARD: Eugenia Laverne Fisher. Police captain, internal security. Scar on lower left leg. Clean driving licence. Last purchase: book, *How to Open a Restaurant.* One dependent daughter, aged three.

Heart beat stops. FISHER is left on her own staring out.

'VERIFIED' flashes up on the monitors/spoken by card.

The Card image on the back dims and FISHER looks vulnerable, uncertain, lost. In a preoccupied daze she walks off stage.

SCENE 12

The Tomlin house. ABI is examining and polishing some 'antiques'. There's a frying pan, an old television aerial and a large rug rolled up. MARCUS is at his laptop. ABI is holding the old kitsch TV aerial.

ABI: Where shall I put this?

MARCUS: In the bin.

ABI: It's an antique. I paid good money for it.

MARCUS: You used to do normal shopping

ABI: I used to be able to go to normal shops. Until I get my new ID I have to use cash or barter with goods.

MARCUS: You haven't been bartering my CDs, have you?

ABI: Only the ones I don't like. I've run out of cash.

MARCUS: Why didn't you say?

ABI: Because I manage.

MARCUS: You don't have to just manage. I'll get some cash for you.

ABI: I have to be able to look after myself.

MARCUS: Why? Don't you want my help?

ABI: I do actually, the cold tap in the kitchen has been dripping. It's a precious resource we're wasting.

MARCUS: Phone a plumber. Probably only a washer.

ABI: I'm not calling out a plumber. We've just had the plumbers in.

MARCUS: Have we?

ABI: We paid a fortune. Get them back.

MARCUS looks confused.

You do remember?

MARCUS: (*It dawns on him.*) Yes…yes… I'll get onto them immediately.

ABI: Thank you.

MARCUS: David's asked me if I want a knighthood. What do you reckon?

ABI: It's a lovely idea.

MARCUS: Ten years overdue. I think I deserve a sainthood.

ABI: Ask him for one of those instead.

MARCUS: He might announce it on the news. (*He looks around for the television.*) Where's the TV?

ABI: I exchanged it for groceries.

Doorbell rings. The CCTV shows MICHELLE at the door.

MARCUS: I watch that.

ABI: You eat dinner as well. And you can't eat a television.

ABI automatically places her hand on the wall Reader. It rejects her, speaks 'TRY AGAIN'. She sighs.

MARCUS: Open.

It accepts him, speaks 'OPEN'.

Get rid of your own things.

ABI: I have. We ate those last week. Food's very expensive in Coventry.

MICHELLE enters carrying a box. Similar to the one she brought before.

MICHELLE: (*To ABI.*) Sign.

ABI gives her print. She is expecting the box but MICHELLE gives her the letter. ABI is a little surprised her print was accepted.

(*To MARCUS.*) Sign.

He signs. She holds the box out to marcus. He steps back from it nervously and points to where she should put it.

MARCUS: Over there. You open it.

MICHELLE opens the box and looks in, she tentatively puts her hand in and pulls out a leaflet. MARCUS is relieved.

ABI has opened her letter and is studying the new ID card and letter.

ABI: I don't understand this.

MARCUS: (*Reads leaflet.*) 'Local bank raid points finger at Coventry. Kidnapping on the increase. Are your children safe? Come to the meeting. Protect Royal Leamington Spa'

ABI: It isn't addressed to me.

MICHELLE: You signed for it.

MARCUS: I like the Royal bit. I want you to distribute these. One through every door. Let's get this campaign rolling.

MICHELLE nods and leaves.

Is that your new card? About time. Back to normal eh? No more trips to Coventry and no more bartering, thank God.

MARCUS exits. ABI is puzzled, looking from envelope to ID card.

Doorbell rings. She drops them into her handbag. The CCTV shows a nervous ENOCH at the door.

ABI: Open.

It rejects her, speaks 'TRY AGAIN'.

Bloody thing.

Grumbling, she goes out to the door. CCTV shows his eye looking into the camera. CCTV goes off. ABI and ENOCH enter.

You're very prompt.

ENOCH: Am I?

ABI: Don't you have any tools?

ENOCH: (*Unsure.*) No.

ABI: Well it's only a washer. In the kitchen.

ENOCH: Hands are tools, sort of.

ABI stops in her tracks. She slowly turns to face him. He doesn't know if he's said something wrong.

ABI: I've always thought that, too.

ENOCH: If you don't mind getting them dirty.

Beat

ABI: I don't.

ENOCH: Me neither. They can be savagely strong. Or incredibly sensitive.

ABI is realising how attractive ENOCH is. He feels a little awkward by her silence.

ABI: Can they?

ENOCH: You can tell all sorts of things about a person by their hands.

ABI: Really?

ENOCH nods.

What can you tell about me?

She slowly goes to him and holds out her hands. ENOCH takes them gently. She is not looking at her hands but at his face.

ENOCH: You've got green fingers.

ABI: You can see that?

ENOCH: And they smell of Duraglit.

ABI: I've been polishing the brass.

ENOCH looks at her, realising how attractive she is.

ENOCH: We used to have a brass door handle.

ABI: It's very good to touch.

ENOCH: Smooth.

ABI: Soft.

ENOCH: Firm.

A little embarrassed, they reluctantly drop hands. She indicates the plants. ENOCH goes to them.

ABI: I really do have green fingers.

ENOCH: Positively verdant.

He strokes the leaves and listens.

ABI: They like you.

ENOCH: I like them.

ABI is feeling the heat of her rising passion. Fans herself.

ABI: It's hot in here, you must be thirsty.

ABI picks up the watering can and fills a glass with water.

ENOCH goes to look at the Van Gogh Irises print.

She hands him the glass. He looks into her eyes.

ENOCH: Your irises.

ABI: You noticed my irises?

ENOCH: First thing. (*He drinks, looking into her eyes.*)

ABI: I'm Abi. Abi Tomlin.

ENOCH: (*Chokes on his drink.*) Oh God, I'm sorry. I have to go.

ABI: No. What about the washer?

ENOCH: Really.

ABI: You can't.

ENOCH: Thanks for the water.

ABI: At least tell me your name.

ENOCH stops

ENOCH: My name?

ABI: Yes, your name. You must have one.

ENOCH: (*Uncomfortable, unsure.*) My name... Abi... (*He takes a breath of courage.*) My name is Enoch Dawes. Enoch Dawes.

ABI: Hello Enoch Dawes. That's nice. Rolls off the tongue. Enoch Dawes. Thank you for telling me. Please stay Enoch Dawes.

She leads him to a chair.

Welcome to my home.

ENOCH: Thank you.

ABI: Enoch Dawes.

ENOCH: Abi Tomlin.

They smile at each other.

It's a lovely home, very...homely.

ABI: Homely yes, but no children.

ENOCH: That's a relief.

ABI: I'm sorry?

ENOCH: I mean, children, so much to worry about these days. With children. Did you want any?

ABI: Yes, my own ones.

ENOCH: I don't have any chldren.

ABI: Are you married?

ENOCH: I was.

ABI: Divorced?

ENOCH: We were going to have children but...

ABI: But what?

ENOCH: There was a fire.

ABI: No.

ENOCH: Yes

ABI: I'm so sorry.

ENOCH: She was on the zebra crossing and he was on his way back to the station.

ABI: Did she die instantly?

ENOCH: No, she moved in with him.

ABI: Him?

ENOCH: The fireman. And I moved out.

ABI: That's very sad.

ENOCH: So no children. What about you?

ABI: Impossible.

ENOCH: I'm sorry.

ABI: We don't have sex.

ENOCH: Oh.

ENOCH drinks his water down.

ABI: How long have you been a plumber?

ENOCH: Err…

ABI: You work for Mrs Plum?

ENOCH: No. Not anymore.

ABI: That's funny her name is Plum and she has a plumbing company.

ENOCH: Does she?

ABI: You're freelance now then?

ENOCH: Totally. Irrationally and inconceivably freelance.

ABI: I'm a naturalist and ornithologist at the Eden Bird sanctuary. I also used to help out with a mobile library for the disadvantaged, until it was stolen.

ENOCH: Who stole it?

ABI: The disadvantaged. I think it should great foresight, this way they don't have to wait every week for new books.

ENOCH: And no overdue fines.

They smile.

ABI: I've started collecting antiques. Look. This is a TV aerial circa 1980s. This is a frying pan and this a rug.

ENOCH: Very nice.

ABI: I have a bird of paradise in my sanctuary. Would you like to see her?

ENOCH: In your sanctuary?

ABI: I have a photo. I'm off sick at the moment

ENOCH: You don't look sick. You look a picture of health to me.

ABI: Do I?

ENOCH: Blooming.

ABI: I'll get the photo.

ABI goes off. Once she's out of sight ENOCH gets up to leave. MARCUS enters. ENOCH turns and bumps into him.

ENOCH: I was just leaving.

MARCUS: I've seen you before.

ENOCH: The plumber.

MARCUS: Of course you are. One of Mrs Plum's boys. (*Winks.*)

ENOCH: No.

MARCUS: I remember you. The precinct.

MARCUS walks up to ENOCH who is backing away.

ENOCH: It wasn't me.

MARCUS: Did she send you?

ENOCH: No.

MARCUS: You came on your own initiative? That was bold of you. I like boldness.

ENOCH: I only came to see.

MARCUS: Me?

ENOCH: No.

MARCUS: Don't be shy.

ENOCH: I shouldn't have come.

MARCUS: Come here. Come here.

MARCUS steps closer and takes ENOCH's hand. Looks at it.

Do you like hands?

ENOCH: Yes.

MARCUS: So do I.

He places ENOCH's hand on his crotch. ENOCH freezes. Then suddenly runs away. MARCUS tries to catch him.

Playing hard to get?

ENOCH: I didn't come to see you.

MARCUS: You're not after my wife are you?

ENOCH: It's a misunderstanding.

MARCUS catches him. Holds him and breathes in his scent.

MARCUS: You smell good.

ENOCH: No I don't.

ENOCH tries to break away, MARCUS won't let go of him.

MARCUS: It's been a long time. I've been stuck at home for a whole week. Sneaking out's been tricky.

ENOCH: Then tell her.

MARCUS: So she can leave me?

ENOCH: Yes. It's only fair.

MARCUS: I don't want fair. I like it how it is. I like you.

ENOCH falls down. MARCUS falls on top of him. ENOCH grabs the frying pan and whacks him over the head. MARCUS passes out on top of ENOCH pinning him down. ABI walks in with the photo.

ABI: Here it is.

Sees them and screams.

ENOCH: He fell on me. (*Gets up.*)

ABI: Marcus? What happened? What are you doing with my frying pan?

ENOCH: I hit him.

ABI: What for? Marcus?

ENOCH: He was aggressive.

ABI: (*Tends to MARCUS.*) He's breathing.

ENOCH: Thank God. He thought I was carnally interested in him.

ABI: Him?

ENOCH: You. Definitely you.

ABI: Marcus was jealous?

ENOCH: Yes. I'm sorry, it was self defence.

The doorbell rings. ABI is loosening MARCUS's tie and shirt.

ABI: See who it is.

FISHER is shown on the CCTV monitor. Flashes her ID. ENOCH places his hand on the Reader and it accepts him 'OPEN'.

What did you do?

ENOCH: I pressed here.

ABI: You've opened the door. It doesn't work for me.

ENOCH: It's the police.

ABI looks at him. CCTV goes off. They both look at MARCUS.

FISHER: (*Off.*) Mr Tomlin?

ENOCH and ABI look towards the door then to the rug. Instinctively they grab the rug and pull it over MARCUS. They stand up as FISHER enters.

Ah, Mrs…er

ABI: Tomlin.

FISHER: Are you feeling better?

ABI: Much. What can I do for you?

FISHER smiles and nods at ENOCH who does the same.

FISHER: I'm looking for Mr Tomlin.

ABI: Did you try his office?

FISHER: They said he was here.

ABI: He's not.

As FISHER walks around they step over the rug to form a barrier between it and FISHER.

FISHER: New rug?

ABI: Yes. I'll tell him you called.

FISHER: Don't bother.

ABI: He could be quite a while.

FISHER: I'll wait.

MARCUS: groans and begins to wriggle under the rug. ABI and ENOCH yawn to cover it.

Your rug's coming to life. Get him out of there. Now.

They remove the rug and MARCUS sits up.

Mr Tomlin!

MARCUS: My head. Ow.

FISHER: What is going on here?

MARCUS: I fell.

FISHER: Oh, please!?

ABI: I was just about to call an ambulance.

FISHER: You're in big trouble this time. Domestic violence.

ABI: No.

ENOCH: I did it.

> *They all pause to take him in.*

> I hit him with the frying pan.

FISHER: Did you now?

MARCUS: Yes. He's an intruder.

ENOCH: He mistook me for someone else.

FISHER: Give me your ID.

> *ENOCH hesitates, looking at ABI.*

ENOCH: No.

FISHER: It's been a tough day. Do me a favour.

ENOCH: I haven't got one.

FISHER: (*Eyes him suspiciously.*) I need to check. Give me a print.

ENOCH: No.

FISHER: Why not?

ENOCH: You can't force me.

FISHER: You think so? (*To ENOCH.*) Sunshine, I'm arresting you for assault. (*To ABI.*) And you're not off the hook yet.

SCENE 13

The Card image pulsates. Music. FISHER leads ENOCH away. MICHELLE offers her ID card to be scanned. ABI is watching her. Heartbeat.

THE CARD: Michelle Boheme, twenty-seven. Female. Single. Hell's Angel. Visits the Opera. No dependents. Owns motorcycle 750 cc. Job: courier. Good Samaritan. Reads *Biker Today* magazine. Recent purchase: 'Bat out of Hell'.

Heartbeat stops.

Verified.

MICHELLE moves away. Heart beat stops. Music for ABI as she walks into the light. She holds up her palm.

Denied.

Please seek assistance.

A searchlight flashes across her. As she tries to run, the searchlight follows, green beams start firing and she has to dodge them. An alarm sounds.

Illegal request. Report to police station.

ABI runs off, the others clear.

SCENE 14

The Interrogation Room. ENOCH is lying face down over the table. FISHER has her knee in his back with his arm twisted. She admires each of his fingertips.

FISHER: Right loop. Left loop. The coordinates of the human fingerprint. A micro-cosmos of mountains and valleys, ridges and furrows in each little digit. Unique.

ENOCH: You're breaking my arm.

FISHER: (*Lets go of his arm.*) All I want is one tiny print, find out who you are and then I can send you home. Unless Mr Tomlin decides to press charges.

ENOCH: No.

FISHER: (*Getting to her feet.*) I'm getting too old for this.

ENOCH: (*Getting up.*) Send me to Coventry.

FISHER: Hold your horses. It's no fun if you decide your own fate. What have you got against Mr Tomlin anyway?

She walks around him holding her Biometric Reader to his eye without touching him. He ducks and dodges her.

You're protecting someone. Everyone behaves the same when they're protecting someone. But it all falls out in the end. And I'll be right here to catch it.

ENOCH: I want to go to Coventry.

FISHER: Never heard of it.

ENOCH: Then prison.

FISHER: They're all full. And you're not a proper criminal yet. I don't know what you are.

ENOCH: I hit a man with a frying pan.

FISHER: Bad boy.

ENOCH: He was after me.

FISHER: Mr Tomlin does have specific tastes. No reason to knock him out though.

ENOCH: I'm a danger to the public.

FISHER: You're a pussycat.

ENOCH: I'm a menace.

FISHER: You don't like yourself very much.

ENOCH: Not much to like.

FISHER: I like you. You're spunky. Small but stubborn. Place your palm here.

She holds out a portable biometric reader which he ignores.

ENOCH: I don't like you.

FISHER: You don't have to hurt my feelings. Just as well I'm a bloody tough bitch. Do you have a wife? Is anyone missing you?

ENOCH keeps his lips pursed.

What was the name of your first pet? (*Silence.*) You might as well tell me something, get it off your chest. (*Silence.*) Secrets. You're not the only one, we've all got them. I've got secrets. I'll tell you one. I'm just a normal person, like you. Bet you didn't know that. (*Silence.*) I've been known to shed a tear over an old movie, and I've always wanted to have my own restaurant. (*Silence.*) Okay here's a biggy. Ballroom dancing. I go once a month. Incognito, of course. Nobody knows that. (*She imagines herself.*) The movement, the music, the physical contact… (*Silence.*) Do you dance?

ENOCH: No.

She points a remote control in the air and a Strauss Waltz plays.

FISHER: It's a waltz. Designed for the purpose of dancing. Originally invented for people with three legs. Dance with me.

ENOCH: I don't want to

FISHER: Stand up.

He does.

One, two, three. Follow me. I'm the man.

ENOCH: I'm the man.

FISHER: I'm the man.

She leads him off. They dance.

Relax. Let the music carry you away.

They waltz. FISHER enjoys the dance but a sadness creeps in. ENOCH dances awkwardly and keeps his mouth tightly shut.

You seem like a nice person. I can help you. There's somebody out there who wants you back. I'm right aren't I? You don't know what it is to lose someone. The pain, the void of nothingness, the vortex of undiminishable loss. (*She loses her patience.*) What school did you go to? What's your favourite colour? How many ways are there to skin a cat? Is violence the answer?

She violently thrusts him into a chair. Angry. Music stops.

ENOCH: No.

FISHER: (*Calming.*) I thought so. I like to talk, just me and the client. Cosy.

ENOCH: You're a lonely woman.

FISHER: Are you trying to pity me?

ENOCH: It was a statement

FISHER: That's pathetic for a statement.

ENOCH: I am pathetic.

FISHER: You're bloody lucky is what you are. I'll show you pathetic.

She picks up a can of baked beans. Gives it to ENOCH.

Look at that. What is it?

ENOCH: Baked beans.

FISHER: Look closer. Now what do you see?

ENOCH: Baked beans.

FISHER: Describe.

ENOCH: 415 grams. Blue label. Black writing. What do you want me to say?

FISHER: That can of baked beans is actually Miss Claudette Loach from Romford, Essex.

ENOCH: Her ashes?

FISHER: No no, too easy. It's not even her baked beans. Look.

She scans the tin and the information comes up on the monitor. FISHER reads.

Claudette Loach. Single, 31. Job: Primary school teacher. University graduate. Owns one bedroom flat. Born: Romford Hospital. No dependents. Eats sweets confiscated from children.

The words stop.

FISHER: Et cetera. No one knows what's happened to the real Ms Loach. And nobody knows how many unmarried women are being sold on supermarket shelves. You could go into your local and buy yourself a wife, go home and have her on toast. That's not progress as far as I'm concerned.

ENOCH: She's a tin of beans?

FISHER: How many times have you seen a tin of beans teaching a class of kids?

ENOCH: Never.

FISHER: When you think about it, what with the false acceptance, false rejects and equal error rates, resulting from user errors, primary system errors, communications and data flow management errors and external interference, it's amazing any of us have any identity left at all.

ENOCH: I'm a fireman.

FISHER: (*Smiles.*) That's progress.

ENOCH: And a plumber.

FISHER: Busy boy.

ENOCH: And an accountant.

FISHER: Bullshit.

ENOCH: Can I go to Coventry?

FISHER: No! (*In his face.*) I could ship you anywhere I want. But I'm not finished yet. You belong to someone. And I intend to find out who. Catch.

She throws her reader to him. He catches it and in so doing gives her his print. His ID flashes up on the monitors. FISHER reads it and is momentarily taken by surprise. She looks at ENOCH then back to the screen, she accepts what she reads, but not without a hint of amusement.

FISHER: Mrs Tomlin. Why didn't you say? (*Beat.*) You'd better go home, Mr Tomlin will be waiting for you.

He tentatively leaves.

SCENE 15

Music into the precinct, night. ENOCH is walking through. ABI enters and sees him. He tries to get away from her.

ABI: Enoch?

He stops. But can't look her in the eye.

I've been looking everywhere for you.

ENOCH: You shouldn't be out, not round here.

ABI: I phoned the police station. They had no idea who you were.

ENOCH: We mustn't meet.

ABI: Yes we must.

ENOCH: I was wrong to come to your house.

ABI: I'm glad you came.

ENOCH: Nothing is how you think it's going to be.

ABI: That's good, isn't it?

ENOCH: My hands. I wanted to put my hands on you not the washer, not the tap, not the frying pan.

ABI: Yes.

ENOCH: It's all wrong.

ABI: You held my fingers.

ENOCH: Green fingers.

ABI: Like we were one.

ENOCH: We are one. That's the problem.

ABI: I've never met anyone like you.

ENOCH: Neither have I.

ABI: I feel that you know me.

ENOCH: I wish I didn't.

ABI: It's rare.

ENOCH: Not as rare as you think.

ABI: To find someone you feel you've known all your life.

ENOCH: You don't know me.

ABI: I want to.

ENOCH: I'm just an accountant without a job. Not even a proper fireman.

ABI: I thought you were a plumber.

ENOCH: You see?

ABI: It doesn't matter what you are. We've connected. We are connected.

ENOCH: We have to unconnect.

Beat

ABI: Are you illegal?

ENOCH: No

ABI: Why wouldn't you hand over your ID?

ENOCH: I didn't want to.

ABI: I won't judge you. I can't. To be honest I'm in a spot of trouble myself. I lost my ID card, then my personal data got corrupted and now they've screwed up with the replacement.

ENOCH: Aren't you angry?

ABI: Should I be?

ENOCH: (*Getting angry himself.*) Look at me. Do I look like you? Do I sound like you? Do I feel like you? No, don't touch. No touching allowed. I came to your house to see what kind of life Abi Tomlin led. To see if I liked it. You have no idea who I am. Or who you are. You wallow in your ignorance.

ABI: Ignorance?

ENOCH: Passive in your acceptance. Open your eyes.

ABI: Why are you angry with me?

ENOCH: Your paradise comes at a price. It's manipulative and immoral.

ABI: What paradise?

ENOCH: I can't do this. I thought I could but I can't. I don't belong anywhere or with anyone.

ABI: You belong with me.

ENOCH: We're being duped by people we trust. We know what's happening, but up here (*Taps his head.*) we deny it because in here (*Taps his heart.*) we feel safe. Until it happens to you. Until you lose everything that makes you who you are. Every solitary thing. Apart from your memories and the clothes you stand in. Then you panic, you hide, ashamed, you grieve, so much that you do really stupid things to try and make it go away.

ABI: Stop (*She holds his arms.*)

ENOCH: Really stupid things.

ABI holds him. He allows her to hug him.

I've done something terrible to you.

ABI: I forgive you.

ENOCH: Don't forgive me.

He pulls away from her and hands her his ID card. She reads it.

ABI: You found my card. Thank you. Where?

ENOCH: It's not yours. It's mine.

ABI: It's got my name on. Abigail Tomlin.

ENOCH: Look at the picture

ABI: Oh God, I look awful.

ENOCH: It's me. It's a cock up. You and I are one. Merged. It's my fault. I'm you. I'm Abigail Tomlin.

ABI: You can't be. I'm me.

ENOCH: You're somebody else.

ABI: Yes, but I'm still me.

ENOCH: I'm you.

ABI: Then who are you?

ENOCH: Somebody else is me.

ABI: A plumber?

ENOCH: A fireman. Now I'm you.

ABI: How?

ENOCH: I bought you. I wanted me but I didn't have enough money. I'm so sorry.

ABI: Oh my God, then this is me. (*Gives her new card to him.*) I thought it was a mistake.

ENOCH: You're a man?

ABI: You're a woman.

ENOCH: I'm you.

ABI: I'm a Brazilian musicologist with a wife and son in Rio. (*Pause while they take it in.*) I don't even play an instrument. They're trying to deport me.

ENOCH: They can't deport you, I've only just found you.

ABI: Help me.

ENOCH: I'll do anything. Anything.

ABI: Don't me go.

ENOCH: I won't ever let you go.

ABI: Thank you.

ENOCH: I can't lose you.

ABI: I'm so glad you're Abi Tomlin.

ENOCH: I'm not.

ABI: Yes you are. You are. Don't you understand? I want you to be.

He looks at her as he tries to take it all in. She strokes his face.

I couldn't think of a nicer person to be me…you…her… Please look after her. She and I have some fond memories. We grew up together.

ENOCH: You want me to be her? You want me to be Abi Tomlin?

ABI: I do. I really truly do. It's the only way. Promise me you'll keep her safe.

They hug.

SCENE 16

The Tomlin house. THOMAS PAINE is in the room, leafing through some books. Off stage can be heard chanting and general rioting. MARCUS enters, flustered, having walked through a flour-throwing mob. Sees PAINE. He's surprised and wary, not sure if he recognises him.

MARCUS: Hello?

PAINE shows his ID, MARCUS reads and recognises the name. Looks suspiciously at PAINE.

Paine.

PAINE bows with a flourish.

PAINE: Thomas Paine at your service.

MARCUS: What the hell are you doing here? (*Calls.*) Abi?

PAINE: She's out.

MARCUS: She never goes out. Not in daylight anyway. (*Calls.*) Abi!

He goes to look out the doorway for her. Then he scrutinises PAINE.

How did you get in? This house has system 4 high level security. It recognises identity by detecting and matching physical characteristics as linked to the police database. Nothing unauthorised can get passed it.

PAINE: You left the bathroom window open.

MARCUS: (*Unnerved.*) I suppose that riotous rabble out there has something to do with you?

PAINE: Whatever the apparent cause of riots may be the real one is want of happiness.

MARCUS: We can't all be happy all of the time.

PAINE: Do you ever need to riot?

MARCUS: No but if I did I'd be quiet about it.

PAINE: Because a legal citizen can be heard without shouting. But this country randomly selects and spits out certain individuals denying them their legal status. It's totally absurd. Every human being is entitled to the same rights.

MARCUS: Now that's absurd. You for one shouldn't have any, you're a criminal. It was you who broke into the hospital, wasn't it?

PAINE: We have a few fervent radicals who think that direct action is the only path. I prefer to keep the dialogue open but I can't protect you from them indefinitely.

MARCUS: Protect me?

There is a loud thump from the room above them. They both look up.

What's that?

PAINE: That…is someone coming in the bathroom window. It's a slippery bath.

MARCUS hides behind PAINE, scared.

MARCUS: I don't want any violence.

ABI enters dirty and dishevelled, carrying a partly filled bin liner. She stops short when she sees them.

ABI: Marcus! What's going on out there? I've never seen people being beaten up by the police before.

MARCUS: (*To ABI.*) where have you been?

ABI: Stealing carrots from the allotments. It's casserole day.

MARCUS: Can't you use the front door?

ABI: You know I can't. It doesn't recognise me.

MARCUS: (*Frustrated.*) You can't go around leaving windows open. It's dangerous. (*Looks to PAINE.*)

ABI sees PAINE and introduces herself in broken Portuguese. Shows him her ID card.

ABI: Bom dia, meu nome Alberto Oliviera. Formerly Abigail Tomlin.

MARCUS rolls his eyes.

PAINE: I'm Thomas Paine. At your service. (*Flashes his card at ABI and bows.*)

ABI: The Thomas Paine? (*PAINE nods.*) I've heard so much about you. Everyone's reading your book.

MARCUS: We're not.

PAINE: Mr Tomlin. You've worked in the biometric industry for many years, you know its capabilities and flaws.

MARCUS: There aren't any flaws.

ABI: I'm a flaw. It's official.

PAINE: When Coventry was established, requisitioned, it was intended as a stop gap. It was never intended to be the burgeoning community it's now become.

MARCUS: A bloody huge detention centre right on my doorstep.

PAINE: Some members of this community specifically claim their identities disappeared twenty-four years ago on Blackout Tuesday while they were patients in the old Milton General Hospital.

MARCUS: I know your game, I googled you.

PAINE: We believe that, buried deep in the hard drives of your computer system there is data that could point to the original existence of those people as legal entities.

MARCUS: You don't care about those people any more than I do.

PAINE: I demand access under the law of natural rights. This information belongs, intellectually, to the free person who was born with it.

MARCUS: You're a canny politician, Mr Paine, a ruthless self-promoter.

PAINE: I beg to differ.

MARCUS: You want to discredit me by proving that I have manipulated information to serve corporate state above the good of the individual, so that you can influence the collective subconscious, weaken the system and force a change by mass revolution.

PAINE: Mr Tomlin, a revolution is what this country needs.

MARCUS: And thus vindicate yourself and your own illegal activities.

PAINE: For the sake of humanity.

MARCUS: Well it won't bloody work because no one's interested in humanity. They want security. And this is the safest society we've ever had. It's what the people want.

PAINE: The truth is what we want.

ABI: What we want is to get back to nature again. All these arguments, data, revolution, vindication, humanity amount to nothing if we don't listen to each other, understand who we are, why we're here. (*She takes their hands.*) We're human beings living side by side with the phenomena of the physical world on a beautiful planet.

They look at her.

PAINE: Alberto's right.

MARCUS: No he's not…she's not.

MARCUS shakes off ABI's hand. There is a crash from the kitchen. FISHER bursts in looking like she's been in a fight. MARCUS jumps, clearly edgy. FISHER flashes her ID card. They look.

FISHER: Everyone okay in here? We're nearly done outside.

MARCUS: Where have you come from?

FISHER: Kitchen window was open.

PAINE: Thomas Paine at your service.

PAINE bows and shows his card to FISHER. She reads.

FISHER: Thomas Paine. Finally we meet. I'm Captain Fisher. (*She shows him her ID card again. He reads it carefully.*) I take it you're responsible for that non-peaceful demonstration.

PAINE: It was peaceful until you started hitting us.

FISHER: Blame me, why don't you?

PAINE: We wouldn't need to protest if we had proper parliamentary representation and a government that listened.

MARCUS: Your people are illegal immigrants…

PAINE: William the Conqueror was an illegal immigrant.

MARCUS: Thieves, murderers, drug addicts, child molesters, lesbians.

PAINE: Two-headed monsters, witches, stamp collectors, yes yes but we still need proper education, housing, healthcare. Your system has wrecked many lives with its fascist, over-zealous laws and sinister utopian ideal.

MARCUS: What is sinister to you provides personal and national security for the vast majority. That's the way it works.

PAINE: You don't seem to understand, Mr Tomlin, I'm offering you the chance to make amends. You'll still get your knighthood. Probably two.

MARCUS looks closely at him.

MARCUS: There's something fishy about you. Check his ID, Captain.

PAINE looks a little shifty.

FISHER: Yes sir.

PAINE slowly holds his thumb up in the air. Then he dramatically turns it down and places it on FISHER's biometric reader. She looks suspiciously at him. Then studies the Reader.

He looks good for his age. Two hundred and seventy.

PAINE: Man is not the enemy of man, but through the medium of a false system of Government.

FISHER: And his mother's only fifty-two. He was born in Thetford, in Norfolk. Close associate of President George Washington and advisor to Napoleon.

They all look at FISHER waiting for her verdict. She looks back at them.

No, nothing out of order here.

PAINE is further encouraged.

PAINE: The system won't survive Mr Tomlin. Listen to the people.

MARCUS: The people like it. It protects them. Everyone knows where they stand.

ABI: I don't.

PAINE: Sixty million identities all flying around cyber-space.

MARCUS: Wonderful, isn't it?

PAINE: There are back doors in the software, wide open. Bona fide citizens are leaking out. You know it. Your company is constantly trying to keep ahead of it, like the rest of biometric industry.

MARCUS: Rubbish.

PAINE: All fighting amongst yourselves for the biggest contract while the people suffer.

MARCUS: There are no back doors and no one's leaking out.

ABI: What happened to me then? Did you know, Marcus?

PAINE: The security on the central databank is as water tight as a sieve and as permeable as a cheesecloth. If it continues Coventry will be forced to expand and the next stop is Leamington Spa.

MARCUS: The government wouldn't dare take Leamington Spa.

PAINE: Give me the archives and I can stop it.

ABI: Give him the archives.

FISHER: Give him the archives.

MARCUS: (*Angry, almost violent reaching a fevered pitch.*) There are no archives. There's nothing. They were wiped the day I bought the Milton General.

They are shocked. Silence. PAINE is gutted, thrown, by this disclosure.

FISHER: That's illegal.

MARCUS: It was an accident of course.

PAINE: (*Close to MARCUS.*) This isn't the last you'll hear of me.

MARCUS: Get out of my house.

MARCUS goes for PAINE who puts his arms in front of him in defence. MARCUS grabs his wrists.

ABI: Marcus…

MARCUS thrusts PAINE towards the door and as he does so PAINE's bracelet breaks into in his hand. MARCUS looks at it then throws it towards FISHER. She picks it up. She stares at it.

PAINE: Corruption is endemic. If it wasn't, this system would never have survived.

PAINE goes towards FISHER to get his bracelet. She won't let it go. He prises it out of her hand. PAINE looks at its now broken state.

MARCUS: I'm sick of whining, whinging, self-pitying losers.

PAINE: (*Quietly controlled, holding the bracelet in his hand.*) I promise you one thing, by whatever means, fair or foul, my people will have equal political and social rights with due dignity, respect and full citizenship. (*Quietly in MARCUS's face holding up the inscription on the bracelet.*) Equality! Liberty! Fraternity!

PAINE leaves.

MARCUS: Arrest him.

FISHER: What?

MARCUS: (*Sees FISHER slumped in the chair.*) What are you doing Fisher? Charge him.

FISHER: What with?

MARCUS: Breach of the peace, slander, sedition, treason, accessory to burglary? Am I the only one with any common sense left around here?

ABI: Why couldn't you just do the right thing for once?

MARCUS: You're nothing to do with this.

ABI: Yes I am. I may be a simple Brazilian musicologist but I'm being pursued for my links with an international drugs ring and terror group. And now I find out it's all your fault.

FISHER looks at her, surprised.

MARCUS: It's not my fault.

ABI: I don't want to spend the rest of my life in prison.

MARCUS: (*Desperate.*) You won't. Trust me. Just hang on until your proper ID arrives. The system is working. It will always work. We should be proud of what we have achieved in this country.

Music, Handel's 'For Unto us a Child is Born'. Lights change swiftly to next scene.

SCENE 17

ABI takes a central position. The Card image lights up. ENOCH, PAINE and MARCUS watch ABI. She is caught in the green scanner laser beams. Trapped. Lights and CCTV cameras are pointing at her.

THE CARD: Alberto Oliveira. Male. Brazilian musicologist. Wife and one son. Collector of ancient trumpets. Reason for visit: Research on George Frederick Handel and sale of twenty-two kilos of cocaine and supply of arms to known terror groups. Wanted in thirty-six nation states. Prepare for deportation.

Music rises. ABI is scared, she looks to MARCUS for help. He turns and leaves. She looks to ENOCH, but he's helpless. FISHER handcuffs her and begins to lead her away.

As they go she turns and watches PAINE who is now changing into MICHELLE. Once MICHELLE is ready the music stops abruptly and lights up on the new scene.

SCENE 18

The precinct. Night. ENOCH is watching MICHELLE. She runs the bracelet through her fingers. She is more deflated that previously.

ENOCH: The former Mrs Tomlin has gone to Brazil.

MICHELLE: I heard.

ENOCH: She's in a men's prison. What should she do?

MICHELLE: Brush up her Portuguese.

ENOCH: I want her back.

MICHELLE: Doesn't that confuse things?

ENOCH: I love her.

MICHELLE: I'm sorry.

ENOCH: You have contacts. You can help me find a way.

MICHELLE: We all lose people we love. You get used to it.

ENOCH: I don't want to get used to it.

MICHELLE: Sometimes life takes us down unexpected pathways.

ENOCH: I'll do anything for her. Anything.

MICHELLE shows him the identity bracelet.

MICHELLE: ELF.

ENOCH: Elf.

MICHELLE: (*Puts it away.*) Small tokens replace lost memories. Hang on to your memories.

MICHELLE goes to leave. FISHER approaches.

FISHER: Checks.

They hand over their ID cards.

MICHELLE: What's up?

FISHER: There's a spot of trouble brewing. I'd go home if I were you.

FISHER and MICHELLE look at each other as if there's something one of them wants to say. Then FISHER breaks the moment.

Thank you.

MICHELLE leaves. FISHER scans ENOCH's card.

Nice to see you again Mrs Tomlin. I wouldn't have expected to find you in this neighbourhood. Sorry about your friend the Brazilian terrorist. Did he mention anything to you about Thomas Paine? He was at your house.

ENOCH: My house?

FISHER: Thomas Paine, he was wearing a bracelet. Small, silver.

ENOCH: I don't have a house. I'm not Mrs Tomlin. I don't know any Brazilians.

FISHER: It's very important, Mrs Tomlin.

ENOCH: I am not Mrs Tomlin.

He storms off but just before he leaves she calls to him.

FISHER: Mrs Tomlin?

He stops and turns. They look at each other.

Mr Tomlin likes cocoa before bed.

She hands him his card. ENOCH leaves. FISHER watches him.

MICHELLE changes into LISA and waits in her office. FISHER crosses to the office.

SCENE 19

Alien Registration office. FISHER stands, nervous.

LISA: I can't see you without an appointment.

FISHER: I'm in a hurry. I'm on a tea break.

LISA: It's rumoured you don't have tea breaks.

FISHER: And I sleep in a coffin. I heard it. I want your assistance.

LISA: You'll need an appointment.

FISHER: I don't need one, I'm the police. Though I've always wanted to be a chef. Nouvelle cuisine. Little place of my own. But that's another life. Thomas Paine. Who is he? I need everything you've got.

LISA: I can't give classified information without a warrant. Have you got one?

FISHER: No. This is personal.

LISA: Rule twenty-three. Do not mix personal feelings with duty.

FISHER: Fuck rule twenty-three. This is off the record. Please. He had a silver identity bracelet, small, delicate. I need to know where he got it.

LISA: We don't have that sort of information.

FISHER: You've got the lot, don't give me shit. You people can get into any file you want. There'll be a reference to it somewhere, connected to someone.

LISA: Why should I help you? So you can arrest a man for wearing a bracelet?

FISHER: That's right.

LISA: I'm here for people with legitimate problems.

FISHER: Shit, you're difficult.

LISA: You're wasting my time.

FISHER: Ms Grundy, I'm fifty-two. This is hard for me. I have a daughter. It's all in here. Look at it.

FISHER hands LISA her ID card. LISA scans it into the computer. The words come up on the screen.

Favourite food Alphabeti Spaghetti, best friend Lulu. Pupil of Hobby Horse nursery, Height 95 cm, favourite bedtime story Little Bear.

LISA: Three years old.

FISHER: That was the last time I saw her. We were separated on Blackout Tuesday twenty-four years ago. I've searched everyday since. My biggest hope was that one day she would turn up in Coventry. But I keep meeting dead ends. Until the other day, I met Thomas Paine, he was wearing the bracelet I gave to her as a child. I need to know if she's alive or dead.

LISA: How do you know it's the same one?

FISHER: I had her initials engraved on it. ELF.

LISA: ELF.

FISHER: My little elf. She'd be twenty seven now. We've got the same initials. My full name is Eugenia Laverne Fisher.

LISA: And hers?

FISHER: Elise Lolita… Fisher.

LISA: Elise Lolita Fisher.

Lights change. FISHER leaves. LISA gets out her bracelet and looks at it. The card image pulsates. The computers are activated. LISA gets out her phone.

It's time for operation SIN. Secure Identity Non-compliancy. Pandemonium go.

She closes the phone and types quickly, possessed. The computer starts reorganising files. We watch the scrambling of data on the back wall card image and the computer monitors. All sorts of Data. Digits, photos. Very fast.

THE CARD: Eugenia Laverne Fisher. Police captain… Elise Lolita Fisher. Aged three. Orphaned. Lisa Grundy. Lisa Grundy aged three. Elise Grundy aged twenty-seven. Elise Fisher. Michelle Boheme, twenty-seven, Thomas Paine aged 270 aged twenty-seven, Thomas Paine file delete. Michelle Boheme file delete. Approve. Deleted. Marcus Tomlin, divide information. Are you sure? Reassign. Elise Lolita Fisher aged twenty-seven, Task complete. (*An alarm sounds continually.*) Activate. Verify. Program self annihilate, ten seconds. Are you sure? Ten nine eight seven six five four three two one.

During this LISA packs up her few possessions into a box and changes into MICHELLE. At zero the alarm stops and lights come up sharply on the next scene.

SCENE 20

The Tomlin house. MARCUS is reading the paper. ENOCH is standing on a chair dusting the plants while humming, wearing ABI's pinny. MARCUS is listening to him, charmed.

MARCUS: Do you have to make that noise?

ENOCH: I thought you liked my singing, baby.

MARCUS: I do. But you're distracting me. The way you wiggle when you dust.

ENOCH: When was the last time you had a duster up here?

MARCUS: I don't think I've ever had a duster up there.

Beat.

ENOCH: I went to see Aunt Jasmine yesterday. She thought I'd changed. But she liked the fairy cakes.

MARCUS: I've always liked Jasmine. I'm glad you're seeing her again.

ENOCH: I don't know why I stopped going in the first place.

MARCUS: Don't you remember?

ENOCH: No. It escapes me.

MARCUS: She kept on about us having children. At that time we didn't want them.

ENOCH: Really? Well I can't now.

MARCUS: Are you sure you won't change your mind?

ENOCH: Impossible. We're having duck for dinner.

MARCUS: No.

ENOCH: Fell out of the sky over the sanctuary. Waste not want not.

MARCUS: Did you log it first?

ENOCH: Was I supposed to?

MARCUS: You used to log and ID everything.

ENOCH: Did I? (*A sadness passes over him.*)

MARCUS goes up behind him and grabs him.

MARCUS: Abi Tomlin you've never looked so sexy.

ENOCH: (*Pushing him away.*) I've got a lot to get through, I'm interviewing cleaners this afternoon I want the place to look nice.

Door bell rings. The CCTV shows FISHER. She flashes her card.

MARCUS groans on seeing FISHER. ENOCH places his hand on the Reader to open the door. Sound and lights. FISHER enters bright and full of urgency, taking MARCUS to one side. ENOCH continues dusting.

FISHER: A result. I've found him for you.

MARCUS: Who?

FISHER: The cyber terrorist. The man who cracked your Unity card.

MARCUS: Cyber terrorist?

FISHER: The department had a hit last night, broke the network. They've been rounding up suspects all morning.

MARCUS: What network?

FISHER: Paine was right, the national databank was tampered with. All sorts of holes, worms, caterpillars, traitors.

MARCUS: Impossible.

FISHER: The good news is, false IDs are coming to light left, right and centre. (*Quietly so ENOCH doesn't hear.*) You might even get your wife back.

MARCUS: She's already here

FISHER: Your real wife. (*Taps side of her nose.*)

MARCUS: Oh. Is there any hurry?

ENOCH: It's your turn to wear the apron now. I'm fed up of dusting.

MARCUS: Not now.

ENOCH: Well, I've had enough.

He exits.

MARCUS: Time of the month.

FISHER frowns at him.

FISHER: We believe the hackers infiltrated the system via a combination of corruption and incompetence. I've communicated with the ringleader. He's willing to do a deal with you.

MARCUS: Me? This has got nothing to do with me. I said be discreet. What's the matter with you?

FISHER: He'll be here any minute.

MARCUS: He's not coming here, Fisher. I'm warning you. If you're trying to implicate me...

FISHER: He insisted.

ENOCH enters with a watering can and goes to the plants.

Don't worry, as soon as he reveals himself I'll arrest him.

The doorbell rings. CCTV shows MICHELLE with helmet on, she flashes her card.

FISHER: He's here.

ENOCH: Open.

Reader sounds accept beep, speaks 'OPEN'. MICHELLE enters. ENOCH goes to meet her.

MICHELLE: (*To ENOCH.*) Sign.

FISHER: Act calmly and let me do the talking.

MICHELLE takes off her helmet. MARCUS recognises a familiar face.

MARCUS: Her?

MICHELLE gives another letter to FISHER.

MICHELLE: Sign.

FISHER is surprised but gives a thumb print. ENOCH is already reading his letter, his mood brightens. MICHELLE puts her stuff down and begins to change into THOMAS PAINE. They watch her while talking.

ENOCH: It's from Abi… Alberto… She's been given privileges for good behaviour and has been assigned to tree planting duties in the rainforest. Her wife and son visit every week. She misses me.

MARCUS: What about me?

ENOCH: Nothing about you.

FISHER: (*Reads her letter.*) 'I'm glad you could make it Captain Fisher. Kill two birds with one stone.'

MARCUS: Is that a threat? What if he's violent?

FISHER: He's playing games with us.

MARCUS: Is it signed?

PAINE: Thomas Paine.

PAINE flashes his card they read it. They accept what they see.

FISHER: Paine?

PAINE: You shouldn't have destroyed those archives, Mr Tomlin.

MARCUS: Paine. Of course.

PAINE: I gave you your chance.

FISHER: Mr Paine...

MARCUS: You think you can damage the system with amateur hackers? Doesn't hurt me, only hurts you and your cause because you're finished now.

PAINE: So are you.

FISHER: Mr Paine ...

PAINE: I found you a room to rent.

MARCUS: I don't need a room.

PAINE: In Coventry

FISHER: Mr Paine...

MARCUS: I'm not going to Coventry.

PAINE: You don't have a choice.

FISHER: (*Louder.*) Mr Paine, the bracelet? Where did you get the bracelet?

They stare at her.

MARCUS: What's that got to do with anything?

PAINE begins to change into LISA. ENOCH watches her while FISHER and MARCUS argue.

FISHER: I need a proper confession.

MARCUS: The security of every citizen in this country is under threat and you're worrying about a bracelet?

FISHER: He's not red handed yet. The silver bracelet, Mr Paine, where did you get it?

MARCUS: I'm personally going to get you sacked. You're a disgrace.

FISHER: (*Calmly.*) This is my case and I'm following my line of investigation. I'd appreciate it if you'd let me do my job.

MARCUS: You're a fucking idiot.

LISA: Lisa Grundy.

They notice her. She flashes another card. They read it.

ENOCH: From Customer services?

LISA: Mrs Tomlin.

FISHER: Lisa Grundy? Where's Thomas Paine?

LISA: This is yours, Captain Fisher. (*Gives the bracelet to FISHER.*) I'm your man.

ENOCH: You're a man?

MARCUS: Now he's red handed.

ENOCH: Are there any women at all?

FISHER: You found it. (*The bracelet.*)

MARCUS: He's illegally using multiple identities. The motorcycle messenger, Thomas Paine and now Lisa Grundy.

LISA: I confess. I am guilty of manipulating secure biometric data and the necessary re-appropriation of personal information, contravening data protection laws.

ENOCH: (*Gasps.*) You stole identities?

LISA: Rearranged. Like a Rubik Cube, you initially displace squares so that eventually they end up where they belong.

FISHER: Why?

LISA: To help people, lost, forgotten or trapped in the wrong identity.

MARCUS: You were in a trusted position

FISHER sits down, shocked. Holding the bracelet.

LISA: So were you. I was three years old when I was taken to the Milton General Hospital for a routine operation. Twenty four years ago. The day the systems went down. When everything was up and running again an hour later, they found I didn't exist, my files had disappeared, my very identity. When my ID never reappeared I was given a new identity and quickly adopted to keep the damage limitation low. I never saw my mother again. All I had was that silver bracelet. You should never have destroyed those records. You should have admitted you made mistakes.

MARCUS: No hard evidence though.

LISA: You've been so busy making money, sweeping up the so called dirt of society that you forgot to look at yourself. Who are you? Have you ever had to think about that? Where do you come from? Where do you belong? (*Pause.*) I know who I am now.

LISA takes FISHER's hand.

FISHER: Elise... Lolita... Fisher.

LISA: Daughter of Eugenia Laverne Fisher.

MARCUS: Don't tell me you two are related?

ENOCH: It's perfect.

MARCUS: It's touching, but now you've concluded your line of investigation, you can arrest him...her...

FISHER: Mr Tomlin.

MARCUS: Don't Mr Tomlin me. She's a criminal and if you don't uphold the law I'll get you impeached. You'll never see the light of day again.

FISHER: Have pity.

LISA: He's right. An officer of the law must do her duty.

FISHER: My baby. Look at you.

MARCUS takes FISHER's Reader from its holster.

MARCUS: Where's your Biometric Reader? I'll do it. (*To LISA.*) Identify yourself. I am arresting you, whatever your name is, in the absence of a compos mentis law enforcer before this witness…

ENOCH: I can't be your witness, I'm your wife.

MARCUS: You're not my bloody wife

ENOCH: I most certainly am.

ENOCH shows his card. MARCUS looks to the heavens in frustration. FISHER takes back the Reader. Steeling herself.

FISHER: I'll do it.

LISA: After you, Mr Tomlin. If that's your real name.

MARCUS: I don't need to identify myself, you're the offender.

LISA: Everyone has to identify themselves at the request of the police.

FISHER: Or come for a trip down the station. Up to you dear.

FISHER holds out the reader to him. MARCUS bad temperedly places his thumb print on FISHER's Reader. She is puzzled.

Try that again, love

He does and looks at the result.

MARCUS: It's broken.

LISA places her finger on the Reader. FISHER reads the result.

FISHER: Software designer, programmer? Doctorate, ethical computer science and philosophy. Elise Lolita Fisher.

LISA: Now you.

Delighted, FISHER places her thumb on it and reads.

FISHER: Eugenia Laverne Fisher. Chef! Daughter aged twenty-seven.

MARCUS: Chef? (*Snatches the Reader.*)

FISHER: I'm a chef?

LISA: Little place of your own, nouvelle cuisine. As a chef you can't arrest me. In fact, with brand new identities we're free to start our lives anywhere afresh.

FISHER: Yeah? What happened to the old Fisher?

LISA: Retired to Coventry, like the former Mr Tomlin.

MARCUS has scanned his iris into the Reader but nothing happens. He is puzzled and bangs the machine.

MARCUS: Fisher there's something wrong with this.

FISHER: The former Mr Tomlin? That's a bit harsh.

MARCUS: It's one of your cheap tricks, isn't it? When I get this sorted, you'll both be behind bars or worse.

FISHER: Coventry?

MARCUS: (*Getting increasingly alarmed.*) Fisher. I'm warning you.

FISHER: Who is he?

MARCUS: You know damn well who I am.

LISA: Unidentified.

MARCUS: I am not unidentified. This is preposterous, ludicrous. I can't be unidentified. I am Marcus Tomlin.

LISA: It can happen to anyone.

MARCUS: Not me. This is my house.

LISA: I think you'll find it belongs to Abigail Tomlin now.

MARCUS: She's in Brazil.

LISA: No she's right here.

MARCUS: Him?

ENOCH: Me.

LISA: Her.

MARCUS: You won't get away with it.

LISA: And the new Marcus Tomlin will be making decisions regarding your assets, the hospital, your companies. Wherever, whoever he is.

MARCUS: You can't. This is outrageous.

LISA: This is life.

MARCUS: I'll get my lawyer onto you.

LISA: You don't have a lawyer, you don't exist. I have twenty-four lost years to make up with my mother. I couldn't let that go.

LISA and FISHER step out of the scene. MARCUS drops his head in his hands.

ENOCH: Cocoa, dear?

MARCUS looks at him despairingly. He then gets up and appeals to the audience.

During this speech other characters enter and watch him. FISHER now wears a chef's apron and LISA holds a bottle of wine and two glasses. ABI holds a passport and boarding card. ENOCH enters and kisses her cheek, he is dressed in a Brazil football shirt and carries hand luggage. He holds her hand.

MARCUS: My name is Marcus Tomlin. I am Marcus Tomlin. I was born Marcus Tomlin and I own a multi-million pound house in Leamington Spa. I'm a government advisor.

I helped make this country what it is. I've been sent to
Coventry by mistake. I don't belong here. You have to
believe me. I have a life. I am Marcus Tomlin. MY NAME
IS MARCUS TOMLIN.

*His voice echoes loudly as upbeat Brazilian music takes over. MARCUS
exits and ABI moves forward. She offers her palm to be scanned. She
is uncertain.*

THE CARD: Marcus Tomlin, Male. Status: Alpha. Credit rating
good. One wife. (*ABI smiles and holds her hand out to ENOCH
who comes to her. They hug.*) Founder of Unity Electronics.
Government advisor on key identity technology. VIP
special privileges. Fear of snakes. Reads *Financial Times* and
Men on Men. Verified. Marcus Tomlin, cleared for boarding.

They move out of the spotlight, a happy couple.

VOICE: Flight 201, Rio de Janeiro to Leamington Spa Airport,
now boarding. Please have your boarding cards ready.

*Music rises. Characters leave the stage. The screen shows a sunrise
over the sea.*

End of play.